Hope you

Book – by

The oldest Matt

you will enjoy Three

of the Poles.

Page 79

Page 91

Page 119

Kind Regards

Chas Matt

24/VIII/12

FORENSIC
FABLES

England	Butterworth & Co (Publishers) Ltd 88 Kingsway, London WC2B 6AB
Australia	Butterworths Pty Ltd 271 – 273 Lane Cove Road, North Ryde, NSW 2113 Also at Melbourne, Brisbane, Adelaide and Perth
Canada	Butterworth & Co (Canada) Ltd 2265 Midland Avenue, Scarborough, Ont M1P 4S1
	Butterworth & Co (Western Canada) Ltd 409 Granville Street, Ste 856, Vancouver, BC V6V 1T2
New Zealand	Butterworths of New Zealand Ltd 33 – 35 Cumberland Place, Wellington
South Africa	Butterworths & Co (South Africa) (Pty) Ltd 152 – 154 Gale Street, Durban 4001
United States of America	Mason Publishing Company Finch Bldg, 366 Wacouta Street, St F ul, Minn 55101
	Butterworth (Legal Publishers) Inc 160 Roy Street, Ste 300, Seattle, Wash 3109
	Butterworth (Legal Publishers) Inc 381 Elliot Street, Newton, Upper Falls, Mass 02164

with love
william orpen

"O" by Orpen

FORENSIC
FABLES

by

O

COMPLETE EDITION

LONDON
Wildy & Sons Ltd
2006

ISBN 1 898029 87 3

British Library Cataloguing-in-Publication Data

A catalogue record for this book is available from
The British Library

PUBLISHING HISTORY

Forensic Fables 1926
Further forensic Fables 1928
Final Forensic Fables 1929
Final Forensic Fables (Second Series) 1932
Fifty Forensic Fables (a Selection) 1949
Forensic Fables (Complete Edition) 1961

Reprinted 1999 by Wildy & Sons Ltd
Reprinted 2006 by Wildy & Sons Ltd
with "Stick to a Stuff-Gown" by Hubert Picarda
Lincoln's Inn Archway, Carey Street
London WC2A 2JD

Printed in Great Britain by
the University Press, Cambridge

FOREWORD

By Lord Birkett, P.C.

کی

It is to me a very special pleasure to welcome this complete edition of the *Forensic Fables* which were originally published in four separate Volumes so long ago as 1926–32. I have long urged that a collection such as this should be made for the delight of the present generation of readers, and to preserve the memory, not only of a learned lawyer, but of a great English humorist. For I regard the *Fables* as notable literary possessions. They have style and humour of a rare and splendid kind, and they deal with almost every phase of legal life with great insight and understanding. Above all, they present the life of the law with a kindly sympathy for all the frailties of human nature, whether they are exhibited by famous judges and counsel, or by more ordinary folk, who find their way into the courts. English humour at its best is always kindly and the *Fables* are in the great tradition. My four volumes of the *Fables* were inscribed by the author and they now stand on my shelves by the side of *Pie Powder* by J. A. Foote, *As I went on my Way* by A. J. Ashton and *Memorials of His Time* by Lord Cockburn. When Dickens published his *Christmas Carol*, scores of people wrote to him to say that they had placed the book on a little shelf by itself to show their pride and affection for it. I quite understand the feeling, but I have placed the Fables in the very highest legal company to mark my pride and pleasure. Theo. Mathew was a dear friend and colleague of mine, and he loved the Temple and the Courts. He has captured the atmosphere of that wonderful world and set it down on the printed page for the delight of his own and succeeding generations. All these Fables are my favourites, but some make a special appeal such as *The Double First and the Old Hand*, because the drawing of the Old Hand brings an old opponent to life, and recalls the excitements of early days at the Bar. *The Witty Judge and the Bronchial Usher* is a very delightful satire on the judicial humorist of the day; and this great gallery of characters

in the law is presented with truth and charm that gives per-
petual delight. Izaac Walton said when he published his
masterpiece that those who did not like his discourse would
like the pictures. Readers of this collection will like both
stories and pictures, for they blend perfectly together; and
although the dresses of the "pretty young things" have gone
out of fashion, the *Fables* defy the passage of Time. The
Publishers are to be congratulated on their enterprise, and the
present generation of readers on the opportunity to make
the acquaintance of a great figure in the law and in literature.
I commend the book with all my heart.

Birkett.

STICK TO A STUFF-GOWN*

By *Hubert Picarda, Barrister*

ONE day perhaps, and may it be soon, while there are still enough eye-witnesses about, someone should write a history of the Bar between the Wars. In its coverage of the Junior Bar pride of place would go to the most popular junior of that period—Theobald Mathew, known to all in his day (and to posterity) as "Theo", whose wonderful *Forensic Fables* are here republished.

What sort of a man was he? The bare outlines of his life have been drawn many times by obituarists. He was born on December 6, 1866 and died on June 20, 1939 in the city of his birth, London. His great uncle (the Apostle of Temperance in Ireland) was Father Theo Mathew, a name that sounds down through successive generations of the family. His father was Mathew L. J. who was also "father" of the Commercial Court.

After education at the Oratory and Trinity College, Oxford, as befitted a son of admirers of Cardinal Newman, Theo was called to the Bar by Lincoln's Inn in 1890. In his early days he joined the South Eastern Circuit and also interested himself in the Commercial Court on whose practice he wrote a book. At one stage he sat in many commercial arbitrations as an arbitrator, and Lord Denning remembers well appearing before him in those days. But Theo really came into his own in the chambers of Lord Robert Cecil at 4 Paper Buildings, first as a frequently briefed counsel on Canadian appeals to the Privy Council with Sir Malcolm Macnaghten, and latterly more and more as a junior in prominent libel cases. He was much sought after as a pupil master, and in his time had as pupils reading with him: Mr. Clement Attlee, Mr. Stafford Cripps, Mr. Quintin Hogg, Mr. Kenneth Diplock and Mr. Peter Thorneycroft.

His biographer in the Dictionary of National Biography conveys an impression of a junior—for so he remained all his life—who controlled his work flow and was never over burdened. The recollection of his clerk Sydney Aylett, in *Under the*

Wigs (1978), was different and his pupils and contemporaries corroborate the clerk's eye view.

Lord Diplock, in an interview in late 1982 with the writer, recalled his former pupil master with obvious affection more than 43 years after his death. "I was a pupil in 1931-1932 and stayed on to devil for him for about six months afterwards. He had a very large junior practice and was very much the old fashioned junior. By that time he had no commercial work at all and had a large number of pupils. These were lodged in the dog hole (as we called it) in 1 King's Bench Walk. He was a great specialist in libel. His main work was in interlocutory matters before the Masters and he was in the Bear Garden at least three times a week. He almost never went into court without a silk and was led time and again by Pat Hastings and Norman Birkett."

"Master-pleader" was the description of another celebrated pupil, the present Lord Chancellor, in an evocative poem "Legal Ghosts" to be found in *Verses from Lincoln's Inn*. The description was one in which Lord Diplock fully concurred. Yet he remembered wryly that "Pat Hastings had at one consultation with Theo the impertinence to say 'This case has been ruined by the incompetence of the pleadings' ". The charge was absurd. Hastings won the case. But Theo always took the precaution thereafter when they were jointly instructed of seeing Hastings *before* drafting a pleading. For him it was a Forensic Fable with a Moral!

While he was no great advocate (albeit a superb after-dinner speaker) he was a lawyer of great distinction in a distinguished generation of learned lawyers. There are many nuances in *Forensic Fables* which reflect this. And he was a notably cunning forensic technician. As an admirer of Gladstone (as well of Dr. Johnson and Dickens) he achieved a notable triumph in *Wright v Gladstone* (1927) *The Times*, February 4, where Captain Peter Wright had defamed Lord Gladstone's dead father, and was manoeuvred by Theo's stratagems into suing Lord Gladstone for libel, giving the latter the means of avenging his dead father. Mr. Norman Birkett, as the biography by H. M. Montgomery Hyde shows, stole the thunder but the true coup was that of his junior.

Theo Mathew was, and remains still, the finest cartoonist the Bar has known. But his greatest claim to fame was and is his wit. It is the fate of most witty men that their wit dissolves in the

viii

ether. In this generation those who had the joy of hearing Mr Philip Hope Wallace in flood get scant comfort from reading reprints of his reviews. In the case of Theo Mathew posterity is luckier. For *Forensic Fables* (the pun Foibles would have sounded in his ear) and *For Lawyers and Others* give a fair measure of the style of a man who was giftedly "*spirituel*". "He was a most entertaining man" Lord Denning remembers. To Sir Patrick Hastings "he was a man with a mind that saw humour in everything". Lord Diplock elaborates still further: "He was the wittiest man I have ever met: he bubbled over with it. And another characteristic, he did not save it for the occasion. I would call on him perhaps once a week and we would go to a tea shop in the vicinity which we called 'The Ladies' because it was run by two gentlefolk. He had no other audience than myself, but that made no difference. His wit was like champagne, nice at the time but evanescent."

There are, of course, many Theo stories. Lord Diplock recalls hearing a well vouched for story of a meeting of the Newman Society where there was a discussion about the desirability of the Pope taking a more active line in social problems of the day. He poured an appropriate jug of cold water on the idea by his jesting observation "You know, if you are infallible you have to be awfully careful what you say."

Three other characteristics stand out from the memories, written and unwritten of his friends.

First, he had a great love and mastery of language. His writing, as Richard Ludlow rightly observed in the *Law Journal* of July 1, 1939, "like his speech was pointed, and in style approached perfection: he never wasted or misused a word; and it was said of his writing that a phrase could not be altered without spoiling it". Nor was this love of precision confined to the English language. The writer's father, a French advocate and Middle Templer, remembered Theo cross-examining him on the different words in French, through the ages, for false teeth: he luxuriated in the nineteenth century "ratelier" and on being asked in later years how he was, he would assume a mock Racine tragedy style and say in his deep solemn voice: "L'ange de la Mort me frôle de son aile". Now a subsequent generation of readers can judge for itself his unerring aptness of phrase.

Next, he was obviously the kindest of men. A pious Catholic, his acts of charity and "comfortable words" were naturally private; but not unremarked. The man who could dissolve in merriment over "Frothy Bob" Fortune putting out a fire "with a few well chosen words" would link arms with high and humble alike. Lord Diplock, remembering Theo's Requiem Mass at Brompton Oratory, adds an illuminating gloss to the obituary notice by Richard Ludlow. The turn out of senior members of the judiciary and of the front row was remarkable for a Thursday in term time; in fact the sittings of the High Court were postponed until 11 a.m. But, he adds "there was also the largest assembly of bores ever seen, because Theo was so patient with them".

Thirdly, his love of his profession and his Inns of Court shines through his writings with a peculiar incandescence. Although he was a Bencher of Lincoln's Inn, of which he would have been Treasurer had he lived another year, he lunched often in the Middle Temple where he belonged *ad eundem*. There, in Hall, he would start at his table of old men (as they seemed to youngsters in the Thirties) and then at the end of his luncheon, munching a Cox's orange pippin, he would circulate from table to table. His conviviality spilled out of his Inns and into the Garrick Club of which he was, naturally, also a member.

Lord Hailsham who also kindly allowed himself to be quizzed about his former pupil master underlined the point of Theo's love of his profession. In a conversation with the writer, a conversation suffused with the mellow affection felt by all Theo's pupils, he summed up: "Theo was the quintessence of the English Bar and Forensic Fables I consider to be the best book about the Bar there is. I used to recommend all my pupils to read it for that very reason."

Though some have wondered why a man with all his obvious qualities never became a judge "one of those unsolved mysteries of the Law or the Lord Chancellor's office" as the *Law Journal* obituarist suggested, there is perhaps no mystery. He would, from time to time, ruefully declare that solicitors were chary of briefing him because of his books. But the facts belied this. And as a Recorder and arbitrator he avoided levity like the pestilence. His father was a junior, an Irishman and a Catholic. None of those factors was a bar to his preferment in his day. But by the 1920's, the period in Theo's life when he was most eligible, there had been one disastrous appointment from the junior bar to the High Court Bench and, Treasury devils apart, a convention was congealing. He was, in fact, in the words of Lord Diplock "a stuff-gownsman *par excellence*". And none the lesser for that. No junior has been remembered with such affection by such a roll call of legal talents. His two favourite pupils, and his two most frequent leaders, Sir Patrick Hastings and Lord Birkett have all recorded their pride in their association with him.

He was assuredly "The Established Junior who had nothing to complain of" (*Forensic Fables*, p 255). And for those who knew him personally, and for those who, like the writer, were too young to know him, his pleasant voices, his nightingales live on.

*NEW LAW JOURNAL   December 23, 1982

TABLE OF CONTENTS

xiii

xvii

TABLE OF STATUTES

TABLE OF CASES CITED

THE COMMON LAW LEADER AND THE
PROMISING EQUITY JUNIOR

THE COMMON LAW LEADER
AND
THE PROMISING EQUITY JUNIOR

‹›

A PROMISING Equity Junior, who had been a Senior Classic in the Sixties, once Found himself Briefed with an Eminent Common Law Leader. It was a Witness Action. During the Luncheon Interval the Eminent Leader Discovered that he had a More Important Case to Attend to Elsewhere. So he Told his Junior Quite Distinctly What Questions he must Put to the Witnesses in Cross-Examination and What Cases he must Cite to the Judge. Owing to Increasing Deafness the Promising Junior was Unable (Despite his Ear-Trumpet) to Hear What the Eminent Common Law Leader was Talking About; but he Wisely Pretended that the Fact was Otherwise. He was an Intelligent Old Bird.

Was the Promising Equity Junior's Performance a Failure? Not at all. He did not Cross-Examine Anybody or Call the Attention of the Judge to the Relevant Authorities; but, when the Plaintiff's Evidence was Concluded, Submitted Successfully that there was No Case for the Defendant to Answer.

Moral.—*The Unexpected Often Happens.*

THE INEXPERIENCED ADVOCATE AND THE
HOLDER IN DUE COURSE

THE INEXPERIENCED ADVOCATE
AND
THE HOLDER IN DUE COURSE

∽

AN Inexperienced Advocate was once Requested by a Learned Friend to "Devil" a Short Cause. As he had Never Raised his Voice in Court (except to Apply for a Case to Stand Out of the List till next Sittings, Keeping its Place) the Inexperienced Advocate was Rather Alarmed at the Prospect. But, being Ambitious, he Agreed to Do his Best. He Gathered that he was to Appear for the Defendant, and that the Plaintiff was the Holder in Due Course of a Bill of Exchange. Also that he was to Knock the Plaintiff About a Bit in Cross-Examination. Pulling himself Together he Went into Court and the Case was Soon Called on. The Plaintiff had a slightly Red Nose and his Linen was not Unimpeachable, but he gave his Evidence Clearly and in a Firm Voice. When he Rose to Cross-Examine the Plaintiff, the Inexperienced Advocate Shook Very Much, Particularly at the Knees, and the Court seemed to be Spinning Round and Round. The Judge and the Plaintiff Completely Disappeared from his Vision and were Replaced by Strangely-Coloured Sparks and Chaos. His Jaw Dropped and his Eye was Glazed. He Became Unconscious of his Surroundings. The Plaintiff was so Horrified by the Inexperienced Advocate's Appearance that he

3

Completely Lost his Nerve. Asking in Faltering Tones what he was Looking at him like That for, the Plaintiff Added that he had been a Respectable Man Ever Since————. Here he Paused. But the Judge Took up the Running, and Before the Inexperienced Advocate had Recovered his Senses, the Plaintiff had Admitted that he had been Convicted of Fraud on Divers Occasions, and the Judge had Given Judgment (with Costs) for the Defendant. The Defendant's Solicitor was so Delighted with what he Regarded as a Splendid Histrionic Display that he thereafter Showered Briefs upon the Inexperienced Advocate.

Moral.—*Silence is Golden.*

THE YOUTHFUL BARRISTER AND THE
EXCEEDINGLY PAINFUL CASE

THE YOUTHFUL BARRISTER
AND
THE EXCEEDINGLY PAINFUL CASE

∽

A YOUTHFUL Barrister was Briefed at The Assizes to Appear for the Prisoner in an Exceedingly Painful Case. He did not Know Much about That Sort of Thing, and was Naturally Rather Anxious. In Particular he Dreaded the Necessary Interview with the Accused. He felt it was Pretty Certain that she would be Overwhelmed with Misery and Shame, and Too Much Distressed to Tell her Sad Story. And he was Sure that she would Look Just Like *Effie Deans* or *Hetty Sorrel*.

The Youthful Barrister had a Very Pleasant Surprise. When he Went Down to the Cells he was Confronted by a Smart Young Person who Appeared to be in the Best of Health and Spirits. She Wore a Fur-trimmed Coat and Sun-Burn Stockings, and Carried both a "Chubby" and a Vanity Bag. Her Nose was Powdered. It was Clear that she did not Feel her Position Acutely, or View the Forthcoming Trial with Any Great Degree of Apprehension. And her Confidence was not Misplaced. For, although the Youthful Barrister's Speech was Long and Incoherent, the Jury Acquitted the Young Person without Leaving the Box.

Moral.—*Keep Smiling.*

7

THE CIRCUITEER AND THE NICE OLD BUFFER

THE CIRCUITEER
AND
THE NICE OLD BUFFER

∽

A CIRCUITEER, Recently Elected to the Bar Mess, Determined to Try his Luck at the Assizes. Arriving at the Railway Terminus Rather Late, he Just had Time to Fling himself into a Carriage as the Train Steamed Out. It was Occupied by an Elderly Party, whom the Circuiteer Diagnosed as a Nice Old Buffer. He had a Rug over his Knees and he Wore a Top Hat. He was Smoking an Excellent Cigar. The Nice Old Buffer Appeared to be Rather Surprised at the Circuiteer's Intrusion; but the Latter, being of a Chatty and Affable Disposition, Soon Put him at his Ease. Before Long the Nice Old Buffer had Offered the Circuiteer a Cigar and they were Getting on Like a House on Fire. The Circuiteer Told him about his University Career, his Uncle Thomas, the Man he had Read With in Chambers, and a Lot of Other Things. Turning to the Object of his Travels, he Mentioned to the Nice Old Buffer that he was Going to the Assizes; that Mr. Justice Stuffin was the Presiding Judge; but that the Profession did not Think Much of him. Stuffin said the Circuiteer, would Never have got a Judgeship on his Merits; but he had Married a Woman with a good Deal of Money and had a Safe Tory Seat. He was just Going to Tell the Nice Old Buffer what

9

the Court of Appeal had Said the Other Day about One of Stuffin's Judgments when the Train Arrived at its Destination. There were Javelin-Men and Trumpeters on the Platform, together with the High Sheriff of the County and his Chaplain. They had Come to Meet the Judge. Sick with Horror, the Circuiteer became Aware from the Demeanour towards his Travelling Companion that the Nice Old Buffer was Stuffin, J. He Made up his Mind Then and There that he had Better Adopt Some Other Profession, and Caught the First Train Back to London. He is Now a Stockbroker, and Doing Very Well Indeed in the Industrial Market.

Moral.—*Take Care*.

THE TACTFUL MAGISTRATE AND THE MUCH-
RESPECTED COLLEAGUE

THE TACTFUL MAGISTRATE AND
THE MUCH-RESPECTED COLLEAGUE

∾

A TACTFUL Magistrate who had Dined Very Comfortably the Night Before with a Much-Respected Colleague (to Meet Several Old Friends) Took his Seat Punctually at Ten-Thirty to Deal with the Business of the Day. The First of the Drunk-and-Disorderlies to Meet his Astonished Gaze was his Host of Last Night. It Seemed that, After Taking Leave of his Guests, the Much-Respected Colleague had Continued his Merry-Making Elsewhere into the Small Hours of the Morning. His Contact with the Police had Occurred in the Neighbourhood of Vine Street at Three O'clock A.M. It likewise Appeared that in a Burst of Mistaken Confidence he had Given his Real Name and Address to the Officer in Charge. The Situation was Distinctly Awkward. The Tactful Magistrate did not Lose his Head. Sternly Addressing the Culprit as John Marmaduke Bundlepump (a Name which Occurred to him on the Spur of the Moment), he Told the Much-Respected Colleague that his Attempt to Conceal his Identity, Based as it was upon a Superficial Facial Resemblance to a Public Servant of Unblemished Reputation, was as Mean as it was Dishonest; and that in All the Circumstances he Could not Inflict a Smaller Penalty than a Fine of Ten Pounds. The Defendant must also Pay the Doctor's Fee. He Hoped it would be a Warning. It was.

Moral.—*Be Prepared for Everything.*

THE DOUBLE-FIRST AND THE OLD HAND

THE DOUBLE-FIRST AND
THE OLD HAND

∽

A DOUBLE-FIRST, whose Epigrams were
Quoted in Every Common-Room of the
University, became Weary of Tuition and went
to the Bar. His Friends were Satisfied that he was
Bound to become in the Near Future either Prime
Minister or Lord Chancellor. They Doubted, how-
ever, whether Either of these Jobs Afforded Sufficient
Scope for his Splendid Abilities. Shortly after his
Call, a Near Relative Provided him with a Brief. He
was to Appear for a Public Authority which Owned
a Tram-Car. The Plaintiff was a Young Lady who
had Sustained Injuries while being Carried Thereon
from her Place of Residence to her Place of Business.
Her Story, as Set Forth in the Statement of Claim, was
that the Conductor, without Any or Alternatively
Sufficient Warning, had Rung the Bell whilst she was
Stepping off the Vehicle, and that by Reason of his
Said Negligence she had Fallen Heavily in the Road,
Abraded her Shin-Bone, and Suffered from Shock
and Other Discomforts. Her Claim (including Extra
Nourishment and Various Items of Special Damage)
Totalled 583*l.* 4*s.* 9*d.* The Double-First had Little
Doubt that the Claim was Grossly Exaggerated, if
not Actually Dishonest. He was Confident of Victory.
When he Got into Court the Double-First found
himself Opposed by an Old Hand of Unrivalled

Experience in that Class of Action. He Looked Harmless Enough, and the Double-First Felt no Alarm. But Strange Things Soon Happened. The Old Hand Conducted the Case for the Plaintiff in a Manner which Shocked the Double-First Exceedingly. After the Jury had been Sworn he Informed his Solicitor-Client in a Whisper which could be Heard in the Central Hall that he would not Settle for Less than Five Hundred, and he Asked the Double-First in Stentorian Tones, with Reference to the Plan, whether he would Agree (1) the Exact Spot where the Pool of Blood was Found, and (2) the Precise Locality where the Conductor had Admitted to the Policeman that he had Done the Same Thing on Another Occasion. When the Double-First Cross-Examined the Plaintiff, the Old Hand Asked the Judge to Protect his Client from Insult; and when he Addressed the Jury the Old Hand Repeatedly Begged that he would not Deliberately Misrepresent the Evidence. The Double-First Struggled against these Tactics in Vain. In his Final Speech, the Old Hand Reminded the Jury of the Possibility that Tetanus or Paralysis might Hereafter Supervene, and the Certainty that a Disfigured Tibia would Seriously Impair the Plaintiff's Matrimonial Prospects. Apart from his Successful Application for a Stay of Execution on the Ground that the Damages (1,000*l.*) were Excessive, the Double-First had a Disastrous Day.

Moral.—*Despise not Your Enemy*.

THE TWO AGED CONVEYANCERS AND
THE GOOD STORY

THE TWO AGED CONVEYANCERS
AND THE GOOD STORY

∽

TWO Aged Conveyancers (who were also Equity Draftsmen) Lunched Together at the Megatherium Club to Celebrate the Sixtieth Anniversary of Their Call to the Bar. One was Eighty-Two and the other was Eighty-Three.

They did themselves Very Well. After a Second Old Brandy Both Felt Mellow and Comfortable and Ready for Frivolous Conversation. So They Told each other Merry Stories of the Good Old Days. Eighty-Two reminded Eighty-Three of the Humorous Observation Made by Old Buffle when the Originating Summons was Called On in the Vice-Chancellor's Court Out of Its Turn; Eighty-Three (not to be Outdone) Recalled the Pun Made by Snorter in the Debenture-Holders' Action; and Eighty-Two Retaliated with the Anecdote of the Solicitor's Clerk who Mixed Up the Draft Affidavits of the Spinster Executrix and the *Feme Coverte*.

Then they Turned to Modern Times, and Eighty-Three Opined that on the Whole the Funniest Thing he Remembered was his Pupil's Opinion in the Ejectment Action. Shaking with Laughter, he told Eighty-Two that the Pupil had Advised that the Trustees of the Marriage Settlement should be Joined as Defendants in the Alternative. Eighty-Two's Appreciation of the Story was so Noisy that Several Members Woke Up and Looked at Both of Them Angrily. And so a Happy Afternoon Came to an End.

Moral.—*A Joke's a Joke.*

THE ZEALOUS CLERK WHO OVERDID IT

20

THE ZEALOUS CLERK WHO
OVERDID IT

∽

A SILK, whose Professional Activities were not as Extensive as they had been, was Sitting in his Chambers Contemplating Some Venerable Papers which Represented Struggles of the Past. He was Immensely Cheered when his Zealous Clerk Informed him that an Old Client had Turned Up with a Brief. The Zealous Clerk Confided to the Silk that he Thought he could get it Marked Up to Twenty-Five. The Silk Directed that the Old Client should be Shown In At Once. The Old Client Said he was Afraid it was a Small Affair, but he would be Greatly Obliged if the Silk would Give it his Personal Attention. It was a Common Jury, Fixed for Next Monday. The Silk, Winking Slightly at his Zealous Clerk, Asked him to Look at the Book and See what his Engagements were for that Day. The Zealous Clerk Produced a Large Diary, Scanned it with Attention, and Found that Monday was Free, Except for the Privy Council Case, which would Probably not be Reached, a Special Jury, which he was Sure Sir John would Agree to Adjourn, and the Part-Heard before the War Compensation Court, in which they had a Capable Junior. These Causes and Matters Existed Only in the Imagination of the Zealous Clerk; but he Hoped they would Create a Favourable Impression on the Mind of the Old Client. Unfortunately the Old Client was so Startled to Hear of the Many Calls upon the Time of the Silk that he Took the Brief Away and Delivered it to Somebody Else.

Moral.—*Draw It Mild.*

THE JUDGE WHO CLOSED HIS EYES

THE JUDGE WHO CLOSED HIS EYES

~

A JUDGE of Considerable Experience was Trying on a Summer's Day a Case of Unexampled Dullness. Counsel for the Plaintiff was Opening. He Continued to Cite to the Judge a Multitude of Authorities, including the Well-known Decision of the House of Lords in *The Overseers of the Parish of Criggleswick* v. *The Mudbank-super-Mare Docks and Harbour Board Trustees and Others,* and the Judge was Satisfied that he had Never been So Bored in the Whole Course of his Professional Life. At about Three-Thirty P.M. the Judge Allowed his Attention to Wander Slightly, as he Felt Sure that Counsel for the Plaintiff would not have Finished his Opening at the Rising of the Court. Five minutes Later he Fell into a Gentle Doze Which Soon Developed into a Profound Sleep. He was Aroused at Four O'clock by the Sudden Cessation of Counsel's Droning and the Cries of "Silence" with which the Usher Preluded the Coming Judgment. The Case was Over, and the Judge had no Notion what Counsel for the Defendants had been Talking about. Was the Judge Dismayed? Not at all. He Assumed a Look of Lively Intelligence and Said that, as he had Formed a Clear Opinion, no Useful Purpose would be Served by his Reserving his Judgment. He Admitted that During the Course of the Excellent Arguments which had been Addressed to him his Opinion had Wavered.

But, After All, the Broad Question was whether the Principle so Clearly Stated in the House of Lords in *The Overseers of the Parish of Criggleswick* v. *The Mudbank-super-Mare Docks and Harbour Board Trustees and Others* Applied to the Facts of the Present Case. On the Whole, despite the Forceful Observations Made on Behalf of the Defendants, to which he had Paid the Closest Attention, he Thought it Did. It was Therefore Unnecessary that he should Discuss a Variety of Topics which, in the View he Took, Became Irrelevant. There would, accordingly, be Judgment for the Plaintiffs, with Costs; but, as the Matter was One of Great Public Interest, there would be a Stay of Execution on the Usual Terms. The Judgment, which was Appealed Against in Due Course, was Affirmed both in the Court of Appeal and the House of Lords; the Lord Chancellor Commenting, in the Latter Tribunal, on the Admirably Succinct Manner in which the Experienced Judge had Dealt with a Complicated and Difficult Problem.

Moral.—*Stick to the Point.*

THE ELDERLY JUNIOR AND THE
LADY PUPIL

THE ELDERLY JUNIOR AND
THE LADY PUPIL

෨

AN Elderly Junior with a Substantial and In-
creasing Practice was Surprised One Afternoon
to be Told that a Lady Wished to See him.
Her Visiting-Card Supplied the Information that her
Name was Miss Jones, and that she had an Impressive
Address in the Neighbourhood of Hyde Park. The
Elderly Junior had no Notion What she Wanted, but
Requested the Clerk to Show her In. On Entering
the Elderly Junior's Room, Miss Jones Smiled Very
Pleasantly at him and Asked Whether he Could
Possibly Manage to Take a Lady Pupil. She Added
that it Would be Sweet of him to Say Yes.

Her Appearance and Manner Appealed Strangely to
the Elderly Junior. In fact, they Captivated him.
He did not Care about Lady Pupils, but he Felt Sure
that he had Never Seen so Attractive an Individual as
Miss Jones. Her Figure was Elegant and her Eyes
were Exceedingly Nice. Particularly so when she
Held her Head Down and Looked through her Eye-
lashes in an Upward Direction. He was a Single
Man.

The Elderly Junior Begged Miss Jones to be Seated.
They Soon were in the Thick of a Delightful Con-
versation, and the Elderly Junior was Overjoyed when
Miss Jones said she would Like a Cup of Tea Very
Much Indeed. The Elderly Junior said he was Sorry

There were only Three Digestive Biscuits Left in the Tin, but Miss Jones Assured him that It Didn't Matter a Bit. She Took a Second Cup of Tea and Ate all the Digestive Biscuits, and the Elderly Junior became so Much Excited by the Whole Affair that he Quite Forgot his Five-Thirty Appointment.

As she Continued to Converse, the Elderly Junior Began to Envisage every Sort of Romantic Possibility, and Determined that he would Receive, at Any Rate, One Lady Pupil. When the Interview had Lasted Almost an Hour Miss Jones said she was Afraid she Must be Going Now, and did he Think he Could Give her a Favourable Answer? The Elderly Junior, by this Time in a Complete Twitter, Replied Gallantly that he Could not Refuse Any Request which Miss Jones might Make, and Enquired When she would Like to Come. "The Sooner," he Added, "the Better"; Slightly Pressing (as he Said these Words) Miss Jones' Well-Shaped Hand. Miss Jones Laughed Merrily, and Said she was Afraid she had been Awfully Silly. She Ought to have Explained that she was Only a Messenger on Behalf of her Aunt Jane, who had Recently been Appointed a Female Sanitary Inspector and Desired to be Called to the Bar. But, of Course, that would not Make any Difference, would it? The Elderly Junior Answered in a Weak Voice that it would Not, and Off Tripped Miss Jones.

Aunt Jane Presented herself the Following Monday and the Worst Fears of the Elderly Junior were Realised.

He is Still Single.

Moral.—*Be Circumspect*.

**THE ENTHUSIASTIC BEGINNER WHO
THOUGHT BETTER OF IT**

THE ENTHUSIASTIC BEGINNER WHO
THOUGHT BETTER OF IT

∽

AN Enthusiastic Beginner was Overjoyed to Receive a Brief in a Privy Council Case. The Appeal had to do with a Right of Way, a Second Mortgage, an Emphyteutic Lease and the Doctrine of the Lost Grant. It Bristled with Points of Interest and Difficulty. There had been Great Difference of Opinion in the Lower Courts. It was the Chance of a Lifetime. The Enthusiastic Beginner Quickly Set to Work to Master the Instructions and Make a Careful Note of the Facts and the Authorities. It Became Quite Clear to him that if the Argument were Properly Presented the Appellant was Bound to Succeed. He Bitterly Regretted that the Etiquette of the Profession Prevented him from Opening the Appeal, but Remembered that, however Feeble the Performance of his Leader might be, he could Put Everything Right by Adding a Few Trenchant and Luminous Words on his Own Account. First, he would Summarise the Authorities in Three Legal Propositions; Secondly he would put the Estoppel Point; Thirdly, he would Laugh the Case for the Respondent out of Court. The Appeal Came On. Five Elderly Gentlemen Seated at a Circular Table Listened to the Leader, who Addressed them in Conversational Tones. It was Obvious to the Enthusiastic Beginner that the Leader was Making a

Mess of it, and that the Elderly Gentlemen were Against him. He Longed to Drag the Leader from his Place and Show him How to Do it. During the Luncheon Interval the Leader Said he would Soon Run Down now, and he Hoped the Enthusiastic Beginner would Follow him. When they Got Back into the Council Chamber the Enthusiastic Beginner Felt Rather Uneasy. His Enthusiasm had Abated. He did not Like the Look of the Old Gentleman on the Left, and the One in Spectacles had a Nasty Way of Putting Questions which Could not Readily be Answered. The Enthusiastic Beginner Thought he would Content himself with the Three Legal Propositions, and Leave Out the Estoppel Point and the Ridicule of the Respondent's Case. A Few Minutes Later he Came to the Conclusion that the Leader had not Done it So Badly After All, and that he had Better Condense the Three Legal Propositions into One. When at Last the Leader Sat Down, the Enthusiastic Beginner Informed their Lordships, in a Weak Voice, that he had Nothing to Add.

Moral.—*Second Thoughts are Best.*

THE WITTY JUDGE AND THE
BRONCHIAL USHER

THE WITTY JUDGE AND THE
BRONCHIAL USHER

∽

A WITTY Judge, while Perusing the Depositions for the Forthcoming Sessions at the Old Bailey, Saw the Chance of a Lifetime. A Prisoner Bearing the Name of William Shakespeare was Charged with Obtaining Money by False Pretences. It seemed that his Habit had been to Simulate Epileptic Fits in Order to Arouse the Sympathy of Bystanders. His Stock-in-Trade was a Piece of Yellow Soap, which, Diligently Chewed, Produced the Effect of Foaming at the Mouth. This Symptom, together with Gnashing of the Teeth and Rolling of the Eyes, had Convinced Large Numbers of Spectators of the Genuineness of his Attacks. William Shakespeare had Consequently Enjoyed an Income which was Amply Sufficient for his Daily Requirements.

The Witty Judge Felt that if, at the Appropriate Moment, he were to Observe that this Seemed to be a Case of *Poeta Gnashitur Non Fit,* his Reputation as a Jester of the First Order would be Made for Ever.

The case of R. v. *Shakespeare* Came On. Unhappily (as it Proved) the Usher of the Court was a Bronchial Subject. On the Day in Question he was Afflicted with a Severe Catarrh and a Rich and Resounding Cough. Half Way through the Opening of the Case for the Prosecution, which was Conducted by a Counsel of No Importance, the Witty Judge Felt that the Psychological Moment had Arrived. By Way of Preparing the Ground he Asked in an Innocent Manner Whether there was not Once a Poet named William Shakespeare. Counsel Replied in the Affirmative. The Witty Judge was in the Very Act of Loosing Off his Epoch-making Jest when the Bronchial Usher was Seized with a Paroxysm of Coughing which was Audible in Newgate Street. Then an Appalling Calamity Occurred. The Counsel of No Importance, Resuming his Interrupted Address, Said that his Lordship's Question Prompted the Remark that this Seemed to be a Case of *Poeta Gnashitur Non Fit*. He had Made the Witty Judge's Joke! The Court Rocked with Laughter, in which the Prisoner (who was Something of a Scholar) Joined Heartily, and the Reporters Signalled to their Messengers in Order that the Stop-Press Editions might Give to the World the Joke of the Century.

The Witty Judge was Equal to the Occasion. With Austere Dignity he Rebuked the Counsel of No Importance for his Unseemly Levity, and Begged the Press, in the Interests of Decency, not to Allude to an Incident which had Distressed him Greatly.

When the Court Rose the Witty Judge Told the Bronchial Usher Exactly what he Thought of him. He also Took Immediate Steps to have him Transferred from the Old Bailey to the Commercial Court.

Moral.—*Preparation is the Soul of Wit.*

IRENE, HER YOUNG MAN, AND THE
NECKLACE

IRENE, HER YOUNG MAN, AND
THE NECKLACE

∽

IRENE MUGG was a Young Woman of Grit and Determination who did her Bit during the War. The Bit was in a Munitions Factory at 7*l.* 10*s.* a week. When the War was over she Reluctantly Took to Domestic Service. Her Employers were Mr. and Mrs. Tompkyns, of Earl's Court. Finding her Emoluments as House-Parlourmaid Quite Inadequate, Irene Determined to Supplement them. One Evening when Mr. and Mrs. Tompkyns were Dining with Friends, Irene and her Young Man (who had Come to Supper) Made a Voyage of Discovery in the Best Bedroom. Their Diligence was Rewarded. As they had Taken the Precaution of Breaking the Window, Irene's Story that Burglars had Carried off Mrs. Tompkyns' Necklace was for the Moment Accepted. But a Few Days Later the Nasty and Suspicious Demeanour of Mrs. Tompkyns Induced Irene to Send in her Portfolio and Seek Employment Elsewhere. When Mrs. Jenkinson of Putney Applied for Irene's Character, Mrs. Tompkyns Curtly Answered that she was Unable to Recommend Irene Mugg as a Domestic Servant. Did Irene Take this Lying Down? By No Means. She Promptly Sought the Assistance of the Amalgamated Union of Friendless Female Workers and Launched an Action for Defamation against Mr. and Mrs. Tompkyns.

The Defendants Pleaded that the Occasion was Privileged. At the Hearing of the Action, Mrs. Tompkyns was Subjected to a Severe Cross-Examination. Did she Believe that Irene had Stolen the Necklace? She did. Why, then, had she not Dared to Make a Definite Charge Against Irene? Because she had no Evidence Against her. Why had she not Searched Irene's Boxes? Because she Thought Irene would Object. Had she given Irene a Chance of Proving her Innocence? She had not. The Judge Ruled (after Carefully Considering the Authorities) that the Conduct of Mrs. Tompkyns throughout the Affair, Taken in Conjunction with her Admissions in the Witness-Box, Afforded some Evidence of Malice. Filled with Righteous Indignation the Jury gave Irene 250*l*., adding a Rider to their Verdict to the Effect that Mrs. Tompkyns had Behaved in an Un-Womanly Manner. When the Damages and Costs had been Paid, Irene and her Young Man Disposed of the Necklace in the East End. With the Proceeds they Set up in a Licensed House in the Suburbs and are now Doing Very Nicely.

Moral.—*Have a Jury.*

THE DEFEATED LITIGANT AND THE
RASH ATTENDANT

THE DEFEATED LITIGANT AND
THE RASH ATTENDANT

∽

A DEFEATED Litigant was Leaving the Royal
Courts of Justice in a State of Mind which can
be Better Imagined than Described. The Case
had Lasted for Thirteen Days. He had been
Offensively Cross-Examined. His Expensive Leader
had Left the Junior to Make the Final Speech. The
Judge had Said Some Very Disagreeable Things about
him in his Summing-Up. The Jury had Found
Against him on Every Point. The Damages were
Five Thousand Pounds. As he passed down the
Central Hall the Defeated Litigant calculated that the
whole Beastly Thing had Cost him Well into Five
Figures. He Felt it was the Last Straw when his
Solicitor (with a Watery Smile) Observed that at any
rate his Case had been Patiently Heard. But it was
not. As he Neared the Exit to the Strand a Rash
Attendant Approached him and Respectfully Enquired whether he would Care to Take a Ticket for
the Annual Concert in Aid of the Superannuation
Benefit Fund of the Staff of the Royal Courts of
Justice. The Defeated Litigant Gave a Scream like
that of a Wounded Elephant and Let Loose a Flood of
Horrid Oaths which so Startled the Rash Attendant
that he Came Over Quite Queer and has Never been
the Same Man Since.

Moral.—*Don't rub it in.*

THE SOCIETY SUIT AND THE UNEXPECTED
SETTLEMENT

THE SOCIETY SUIT AND THE
UNEXPECTED SETTLEMENT

∽

THE Case of *Potte* v. *Kettle* was about to be
Heard. It was a Society Suit in the Best Sense
of the Term. The Countess of Potte (Married
Woman) was Suing Lady Cleopatra Kettle (Spinster)
for Damages for Slander under the Slander of Women
Act, 1891. Lady Cleopatra Kettle (Spinster) was
Counter-claiming Damages for Slander from the
Countess of Potte (Married Woman) under the Slander
of Women Act, 1891. If the Alleged Observations of
Both Ladies were True, Neither of Them was Fit to
Move in Respectable Circles. The Defence of Both
Parties (Settled by Very Experienced Pleaders) was
that the Words had not been Spoken and/or that the
Words were Spoken on a Privileged Occasion and/or
that the Words were True in Substance and in Fact.
Counsel of the First Magnitude had been Briefed.
Sir Nathaniel (with Another Leader and Two
Juniors) was for the Plaintiff, and Sir Peregrine (with
Another Leader and Two Juniors) was for the
Defendant. The Representatives of the Press were
Sharpening their Pencils. Fashionable Folk in the
Gallery were Telling Each Other to Keep Quiet.
The Judge, in a Pair of Clean Bands, was Glancing at
"Fraser on Libel." The Jury was being Sworn.
One of Sir Nathaniel's Juniors was Clearing his Throat
Preparatory to Opening the Pleadings. The Air was

Charged with Electricity. You could have Heard a Pin Drop. When Eleven Jurors had been Sworn the Associate Whispered to the Judge that One Special Juror had not Turned Up. The Judge, who was a Scholar and an Antiquarian, Rejoiced in Archaic Terminology. "Sir Nathaniel and Sir Peregrine," he said "An event has Occurred which Makes it Necessary, if I am not Mistaken, for One or Both of You to Pray a *Tales*." Counsel Conferred. Sir Nathaniel asked Sir Peregrine Whether he Knew what on Earth the Old Boy was Talking About, and What the Blazes was the Thing he Wanted them to Pray for. Sir Peregrine Replied that he hadn't a Notion, and Didn't Sir Nathaniel Think they had Better Settle? Sir Nathaniel Cordially Agreed. And so, to the Fury of the Countess of Potte, Lady Cleopatra Kettle, and the Public, the Case of *Potte* v. *Kettle* was Settled on Terms Indorsed on Counsel's Briefs, Judge's Order if Necessary.

Moral.—*Talk English*.

THE TRAVELLER WHO SUFFERED FROM
SHOCK

THE TRAVELLER WHO SUFFERED FROM SHOCK AND THE RAILWAY COMPANY'S PHYSICIAN

∽

A TRAVELLER, who was not Such a Fool As he Looked, had the Good Fortune to Escape from a Railway Accident with Nothing Worse than a Slight Shock to his System. But Feeling that the Railway Company might Well be Encouraged to Cough Up, he Instructed his Solicitor to Write a Suitable Letter. The Railway Company Politely Suggested that their Physician should Visit the Traveller and Ascertain the Extent of his Injuries. The Railway Company's Physician Duly Waited upon the Traveller, and Found him Seated in an Invalid Chair in a Completely Paralysed Condition. He was so Horrified by the Traveller's Deplorable Appearance that he Quite Forgot to Ask him whether his Dilapidated State was the Result of the Railway Accident. It was in fact Due to the Negligence of a Nurserymaid who had Upset the Traveller's Perambulator in Kensington Gardens in 1864, when he was Twelve Months Old. But the Traveller did not See why he should Trouble the Railway Company's Physician with these Autobiographical Details. When the Railway Company Offered the Traveller 2,000*l.* in Full Settlement, he Wisely Held Out for 2,500*l.*, and Got it.

Moral.—*Sit Tight.*

49

ADOLPHUS BROWN, MR. JUSTICE GRUMP, AND
THE INTERESTING CASE

ADOLPHUS BROWN, MR. JUSTICE GRUMP, AND THE INTERESTING CASE

∾

ADOLPHUS BROWN was an Amiable Youth of Gentle Manners and Undistinguished Appearance. Rather to the Surprise of his Oxford Tutor, who had Anticipated that he would Fail to Satisfy the Examiners, Adolphus Secured a Third Class in the Honours School of Jurisprudence. Heartened by his Success, old Mr. Brown Insisted that Adolphus should Become a Member of the Honourable Society of the Outer Temple, with a View to being called to the Bar. Thereafter Adolphus Devoted his Time to the Reading of "Shirley's Leading Cases" and the Sampling of such Musical Entertainments as Seemed to Deserve his Support. To Tell the Truth, Adolphus Disliked the Law Exceedingly. When Adolphus was Beginning to Feel that he Couldn't Stick It Much Longer, Mr. Justice Grump (who was an Old Friend of the Family) Proposed that he should Accompany him as Marshal on his Next Circuit. Adolphus Gladly Accepted the Invitation, as it Sounded like a Soft Job. Whilst Travelling in State to the First Assize Town, he Realised that Things were Going to be Pretty Dull. His Prognostications were Well-Founded. Mr. Justice Grump, though a Jurist of the First Water, was not Exactly Chatty. Every Evening after the Court had Risen, Mr. Justice Grump Took Adolphus for a Long Walk in the Country. The One Bright Spot about these Expeditions was that he did not Expect

Adolphus to Converse. But there came an Awful Day when Grump, J., Let himself Go. He became very Talkative about a Beastly Case he was going to Try next Week, and Told Adolphus All about it. As Mr. Justice Grump's Well-Ordered Narrative Proceeded, Adolphus became More and More Confused. The Story Concerned a County Council, a Foreshore, Prescriptive Rights, a Lunatic Not so Found by Inquisition, and a Marriage between a Roman Catholic Spaniard and an Irish Protestant in Amsterdam. When Adolphus' Attention was Beginning to Wander, Mr. Justice Grump Suddenly Stopped and Asked him for his Views as to How the Case should be Decided. Adolphus, who at the Moment was Thinking how Charming Miss Popsie Dalrymple Looked in the Second Act, nearly Died of Horror. His Brain Stopped Working and his Mouth became Dry. He Tried Unsuccessfully to Remember What had been Held in *Lickbarrow* v. *Mason*.[1] He Goggled. Then Adolphus had a Brilliant Inspiration. He Cleared his Throat and Said in a Confident Voice that he would Leave the Whole Thing to the Jury. To the Unutterable Amazement of Adolphus, Mr. Justice Grump Replied that On the Whole he Agreed that it was Largely a Question of Fact. Adolphus Breathed Again. But the Affair had Given him a Nasty Jar, and he Felt Quite Shaken. So Much So that Adolphus had to have Two Stiff Whiskies and Sodas before Dinner, Two more during the Repast, and Several after Mr. Justice Grump had Retired to Rest.

Moral.—*Fortune Favours the Brave.*

[1] 5 T. R. 683.

MR. BLOWHARD, K.C. AND MR. FOOTLE, K.C.

MR. BLOWHARD, K.C. AND
MR. FOOTLE, K.C.

∽

MR. BLOWHARD, K.C., and Mr. Footle, K.C., Stood Jointly on the Top Rung of the Professional Ladder. Whether Blowhard Made more Money than Footle was a Moot Point. Whether Footle's or Blowhard's Methods of Advocacy were to be Preferred was Another. Solicitors Wondered how on Earth they would Get On when Blowhard and Footle were Gathered to their Fathers. When in Difficulties, Managing Clerks Rushed to Retain Blowhard, and if they Found that his Services had Already been Requisitioned, they Hurried to Retain Footle. And *Vice Versâ*. Blowhard was Violent, Noisy, Quarrelsome, Aggressive, and Occasionally Insolent. Footle was Gentle, Submissive, Diffident, Deprecating and Invariably Inaudible. Blowhard Lost an Immense Number of Actions by Getting Up an Unnecessary Row with the Judge. Footle Lost an Immense Number of Actions by his Rabbit-like Behaviour. Their Respective Incomes were Enormous. They Despised Judicial Honours. They Continued to Practise at the Bar long after the Decay of their Faculties had Set In; but Happily those who Briefed them never Noticed the Difference. When they Passed Away, as they Ultimately did, the Business of the Royal Courts of Justice went on just as if Nothing had Happened.

Moral.—*Acquire a reputation.*

THE BLUSHING BEGINNER AND THE
BEARDED JURYMAN

THE BLUSHING BEGINNER
AND
THE BEARDED JURYMAN

∽

A SOLICITOR Briefed a Blushing Beginner to Defend a Prisoner at the Assizes. He Assured the Blushing Beginner that there was no Cause for Anxiety as the Prisoner hadn't an Earthly. When the Jury Acquitted the Prisoner the Blushing Beginner could Hardly Believe his Ears. He felt that he had indeed been Wise to Devote so much Time to the Study of the Works of Quintilian on Oratory and the Great Speeches of Such Masters as Cicero and Demosthenes. That his Address to the Jury had Done the Trick he had Little Doubt. For he had Observed that a Juryman with a Black Beard in the Front Row had Paid Close Attention to his Best Points. Which Particular Portion of his Speech had been Most Effective the Blushing Beginner could not be Sure. He Inclined to think it was the Peroration. For when he had Come to the Bit about the Dawn Breaking and the Sun Gilding the Distant Hills the Bearded Juryman had Shewn Considerable Emotion. Thus Meditating, the Blushing Beginner Proceeded from the Court to his Lodgings in High Spirits. On his Way he Observed the Bearded Juryman just Ahead of him. Hurrying Forward, the Blushing Beginner Wished the Bearded Juryman a Good Evening and Engaged him in Conversation.

"Could you tell me," he said, "without Divulging any Secret of the Jury-box, what it was that Convinced you of the Prisoner's Innocence? Was it my Cross-examination of the Prosecutor? Or the Failure of the Crown to Call Robinson? Or was it, perchance, the Argument which I Put Forward in my Final Speech?" The Bearded Juryman Replied, with Some Warmth, that he didn't Know or Care what the other Mugs Thought, but for his Part he (the Bearded Juryman) didn't See why his Sister's Son should be Sent to Quod even if the Boy *had* Stole a Tenner from the Blinking Blighter who had Done him (the Bearded Juryman) over a Deal Two Years ago. The Bearded Juryman then Expectorated Fiercely and Turned into the "Blue Pig" for Further Refreshment. The Blushing Beginner Gathered from these Remarks that there were Collateral Reasons for the Opinion of the Bearded Juryman which were not Strictly Relevant to the Main Issues in the Case. But he Decided to Treat the Bearded Juryman's Disclosures as Confidential.

Moral.—*Study Quintilian on Oratory*.

THE UTTER BARRISTER AND THE
IMPORTANT TREATISE

THE UTTER BARRISTER AND THE
IMPORTANT TREATISE

∾

AN Utter Barrister was Sincerely Attached to a Charming Young Person, who Reciprocated his Regard. But as his Professional Takings were Negligible, and the Charming Young Person's Relatives Manifested no Desire to Provide an Income for Two, the Utter Barrister Felt that his Engagement was Likely to be a Long One. He was Accordingly Somewhat Dejected. Why Solicitors should be so Coy he did not Understand. For (though a Modest Man) he was Compelled to Admit that he was of Good Appearance and Marked Intellectual Ability. Whilst Engaged in the Soothing Occupation of Smoking Gaspers the Utter Barrister was Struck by a Bright Idea. To Seize Pen and Paper was the Work of a Moment. To Draft an Eloquent Advertisement for Insertion in the Public Prints was the Work of Another. Week by Week During the Ensuing Twelve Months the World was Informed that the Utter Barrister had in Course of Preparation a Treatise in Nine Volumes; Three Concerning the Laws (Statutory) of England, Scotland, Northern Ireland, the Irish Free State and the British Dominions Beyond the Seas; Three Devoted to Public and Private International Law, Conflict of Laws, Jurisprudence and the History of Legal Tribunals; and Three Containing a Complete Digest (Correlated, Analysed and

Indexed) of all Reported Cases on Contract and Tort since the year 1685. The Price (Payable by Instalments) was to be Twelve Guineas Net; Thin Paper Edition, Fourteen Guineas Net. As the Year Advanced the Wording of the Advertisement was Slightly Altered, and the Treatise was Declared to be "In the Press," "About to be Published," and "Shortly to Appear." The Intelligent Anticipations of the Utter Barrister were Realised. Managing Clerks Flocked to his Chambers in such Gratifying Numbers that at the Beginning of the Long Vacation he was Enabled to Lead the Charming Young Person to the Hymeneal Altar with the Full Approval of her Close-Fisted Relations. Did the Nine Volumes Appear in Due Course? They did not. On his Return from the Honeymoon the Utter Barrister, with the assistance of the Press Agency, Broke to the Public the News that Owing to the Carelessness of a Domestic Servant the Manuscript of the Great Work had been Destroyed and that its Publication was Indefinitely Postponed. Filled with Sympathy for the Utter Barrister in this Appalling Misfortune, the Solicitors of the Metropolis Redoubled their Attentions, and the Utter Barrister was so Overwhelmed with Work that he was Shortly Compelled to apply for a Silk Gown.

Moral.—*Write a Book*.

THE COMMON LAW JUNIOR AND THE
ORIGINATING SUMMONS

THE COMMON LAW JUNIOR AND
THE ORIGINATING SUMMONS

∽

A COMMON LAW JUNIOR was Instructed to Appear in the Chancery Division. The Proceeding was Called an Originating Summons. He was informed by his Client that he would not be Expected to Explain the Points to the Judge, as he was to Have an Experienced Chancery Leader to Assist him. This News Comforted the Common Law Junior a Good Deal, for he could not Understand what the Dickens the Case was About. In the Affidavits there were Dark Allusions to an Estate *Pur Autre Vie,* a Gift Over on a Compound Event, and a Failure by Ademption. The Only Thing he could Grasp Clearly was that an Old Woman had Made a Will and Died. When the Case was Called on, the Common Law Junior was told by a Breathless Clerk that the Experienced Chancery Leader was in the House of Lords and that he was to Carry On till the Experienced Chancery Leader could Get Back. The Common Law Junior Rose to his Feet and Told the Judge in Faltering Accents that he would Read the Affidavits. At first All went Well. The Common Law Junior Read and the Judge Followed him Attentively. When the Common Law Junior Turned Over the Judge Turned Over also. But then a Hideous Event Occurred. Towards the End of the Third Affidavit the Judge Suddenly Said to the

Common Law Junior: "But How do you Get Over *in re Puffington's Settlement*?" The Common Law Junior Fainted.

When he Came to himself he was Aware that Three Old Gentlemen with Beards were Asking for Costs out of his Estate.

Moral.—*Ask for an Adjournment.*

THE SARCASTIC COUNSEL AND
MR. MACINTOSH, THE MONEYLENDER

THE SARCASTIC COUNSEL AND
MR. MACINTOSH, THE MONEYLENDER

～

A SARCASTIC Counsel Smiled Grimly as he
Perused his Brief. He was to Appear for a
Borrower (Mr. Algernon FitzCholmondely)
against a Moneylender (Mr. Alexander MacIntosh, of
Jermyn Street, W.1). It was a Short Cause. Mr.
FitzCholmondely had Borrowed a Hundred Pounds
from Mr. MacIntosh, Handing to him at the same
time a Promissory Note for Two Hundred Pounds,
Payable by Four Monthly Instalments of Fifty.
After Paying Two Instalments, Mr. FitzCholmondely
had Defaulted. He had then Borrowed a Further
Hundred Pounds, Accepting, at the same Time, a
Bill of Exchange for Five Hundred. Thereafter a
Series of Complicated Transactions had been Carried
Through, with the Final Result that Mr. Fitz-
Cholmondely had Borrowed One Thousand Two
Hundred and Fifty Pounds, Repaid Two Thousand
Five Hundred, and Still Owed Three Thousand
Pounds, Eleven Shillings and Nine Pence. As the
Short Cause List was to be Taken by a Judge of
Scottish Extraction, the Sarcastic Counsel Felt that
he would Have Some Fun. His Lordship, he
Shrewdly Surmised, would not Sympathise with the
Attempt of a Caledonian from Judæa to Take Advan-
tage of a Foolish and Needy Englishman. The Case
Came on and Mr. Alexander MacIntosh went into

69

the Box. To the Extreme Surprise and Annoyance of the Sarcastic Counsel, he Proved to be a Genuine Scot with a Red Beard and an Aberdonian Accent of Appalling Purity. Whereas Mr. Algernon Fitz-Cholmondely had Relunctantly to Admit in Cross-Examination that he was Born in Warsaw and that his Name was Originally Rosenbaumski. Not Only did the Judge of Scottish Extraction Enter Judgment for the Plaintiff for the Full Amount, but he Peremptorily Refused a Stay of Execution.

Moral.—*Look Out*.

THE AMBITIOUS YOUTH WHO WANTED
ELIGIBLE CHAMBERS

THE AMBITIOUS YOUTH WHO
WANTED ELIGIBLE CHAMBERS

∽

AN Ambitious Youth was Advised that if he
Wished to Succeed at the Bar it was All-
Important that he should Secure Eligible
Chambers. He Accordingly Embarked upon this
Quest Directly After his Call. The Ambitious Youth
was Quite Clear as to his Requirements. He did not
Wish to Confine himself to Government Work, nor
to Tie himself Up in the Commercial Court, the
Admiralty Court or the Old Bailey. What the Ambi-
tious Youth Desired was a Comfortable Room in a
Set of Chambers on the Ground or First Floor where
there were (1) a Busy Leader (of Conservative
Politics) who would Shortly become a Judge; (2) a
Junior with a Heavy Mixed Practice who was in need
of a "Devil" and would Soon Take Silk; and (3) an
Experienced and Active Clerk. After Six Months
had Elapsed he Felt that he need not Insist on the
Busy Leader. When Nine Months had Gone By he
Thought that the Second Floor might Do. A Year
after his Call the Ambitious Youth Closed with an
Offer of Half a Room, the Other Moiety of Which was
Occupied by a Coloured Gentleman. The Chambers
were on the Fourth Floor. The Other Tenants were
a Female Journalist and an Elderly Person who was
not a Teetotaller. The Clerk was an Oaf with a
Squint who Smoked Cigarettes.

Moral.—*Aim High.*

THE WHITE-HAIRED TRUSTEE AND THE
HIGHLY-PLACED OFFICIAL

THE WHITE-HAIRED TRUSTEE
AND
THE HIGHLY-PLACED OFFICIAL

∽

THERE was Once a Dear Old Trustee. He had White Hair and Gold Spectacles. His Reputation for Stability and Integrity Equalled that of the Bank of England. For Many Years he had Enjoyed the Confidence and Esteem of the Various Widows and Orphans whose Affairs and Securities were in his Capable Hands. But the White-haired Trustee, having Rashly Availed himself of Certain Inside Information as to Rubber, got into a Nasty Financial Mess and Came to the Conclusion that he had Better Do a Bolt. He Felt, at the Same Time, (1) that it would be a Pity to Leave Behind Anything Belonging to his *Cestuis Que Trustent* which could be Turned into Ready Money, and (2) that Penal Servitude Should, If Possible, be Avoided. The White-haired Trustee accordingly Placed a Nice Little Lot of Bearer Bonds and Coupons in his Bag, Procured a Ticket for the Continent, and Repaired to Scotland Yard. Here his Admirable Appearance Secured for him an Interview with a Highly-Placed Official. Stating that he had been Robbed, the White-haired Trustee Handed to the Highly-Placed Official a List of the Choses in Action which his Bag Contained, and Begged to be Told where the Thieves were Likely to Endeavour to Encash them. The Highly-

Placed Official Expressed his Keen Sympathy and Courteously Supplied the Desired Information. The White-haired Trustee Thanked him Warmly, and Disposed of the Nice Little Lot in the Cities Named by the Highly-Placed Official at Very Satisfactory Prices. The White-haired Trustee has not been Heard of Since. The Highly-Placed Official has Retired on a Pension.

Moral.—*Melius Est Petere Fontes.*

THE REAL PROPERTY LAWYER AND
THE SURLY GAMEKEEPER

THE REAL PROPERTY LAWYER AND
THE SURLY GAMEKEEPER

∽

ONCE Upon a Time there was a Learned Real Property Lawyer whose Industry and Erudition were the Pride and Joy of Lincoln's Inn. He Knew All About Reversions, Easements in Gross, Registration of Title, and Ancient Lights. In Short, he was Hot Stuff. At the Same Time he was not a Mere Book-Worm. Every Sunday he Took a Long Country Walk in Order that his Physical Frame, Exhausted by the Labours of the Week, might be Recuperated and Refreshed. After a Comfortable Tea at a Wayside Inn he would Return by Train to Porchester Terrace, where a Cold Supper Awaited him. Familiar as he was with the Niceties of the Law, Notices Forbidding him to Trespass under Pain of Prosecution Caused him no Alarm. If Challenged by the Owner of the Messuage or Hereditament through which he was Minded to Pass, he would Point Out that he was Making no Claim of Right, that his Act was Tortious and not Criminal, and that he was Ready to Pay any Damages which a Civil Court might Assess. He Found that the Owner Invariably Permitted him to Proceed upon his Way. One Sunday Evening the Real Property Lawyer, Somewhat Fatigued by a Twelve-Mile Walk, Took a Short Cut through the Deer-Park Surrounding the

Elizabethan Mansion of Sir Moses Blumenkopf, First Baronet. By so Doing he was Making Sure of Catching the Six-Forty-Three Train to Victoria. When the Real Property Lawyer was a Few Hundred Yards from the Highway, he Encountered a Surly Gamekeeper who was Accompanied by an Ill-Looking Dog. Barring his Progress, the Surly Gamekeeper Asked him in an Angry Voice and Highly Illiterate Terms What the Blazes he Meant by Coming on to Land Where he hadn't No Business not to Be. The Real Property Lawyer Adjusted his Spectacles, and Replied that he was Well Aware that he was Committing a Civil Trespass. He Added that he was Prepared to Accept Service of a Writ of Summons, should Sir Moses See Fit to Institute Proceedings in the Chancery Division. The Real Property Lawyer then Drew from his Pocket the Sum of Sixpence and Offered it to the Surly Gamekeeper, Begging him to Note that he had Made a Tender of An Adequate Sum by way of Damages. Did the Real Property Lawyer's Entirely Correct Demeanour Pacify the Surly Gamekeeper? Far from It. Uttering Strange Oaths, he Seized the Real Property Lawyer by the Left Whisker (Causing him thereby Considerable Pain) and Intimated that if he did not Forthwith Retrace his Steps he would Jolly Well Bash his Face In. The Ill-Looking Dog meanwhile Emitted Growls of a Very Unnerving Character. Deeming it Prudent to Close the Discussion, the Real Property Lawyer Silently Limped Away in the Direction Indicated by the Surly Gamekeeper. In Consequence he Missed his Train, was Very Late for Supper, and Incurred the Grave Displeasure of his Housekeeper.

Moral.—*Good Law Makes Hard Cases.*

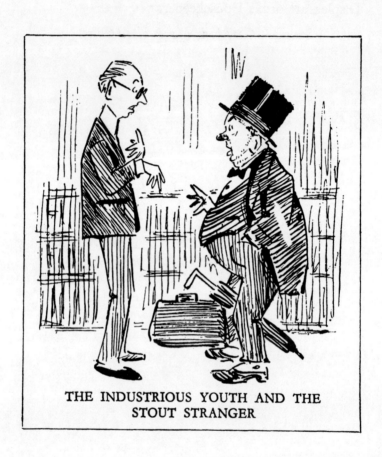

THE INDUSTRIOUS YOUTH AND THE
STOUT STRANGER

THE INDUSTRIOUS YOUTH AND
THE STOUT STRANGER

~

ONE Evening an Industrious Youth was
Sitting in his Chambers Reading the Current
Number of the Law Reports. He was Full
of Hope, but Briefs had hitherto been Rare and of
Poor Quality. Hearing a Knock, the Industrious
Youth Opened the Door to a Stout Stranger. Seat-
ing himself in the Arm-Chair, the Stout Stranger Told
the Industrious Youth that he was Looking Out for a
Capable Junior, and that he had been Much Struck by
the Industrious Youth's Skilful Conduct of a Case in
the Whitechapel County Court. Could the In-
dustrious Youth Undertake a Heavy Job which the
Stout Stranger had On Hand? The Industrious
Youth having Intimated that a Heavy Job would Suit
him Nicely, the Stout Stranger Expressed Extreme
Satisfaction and Said that he would Send the Instruc-
tions Along the First Thing To-morrow. He Added
that he was on his Way to Give a General Retainer to
Sir John, as Money was no Object. The Industrious
Youth Applauded this Excellent Choice of a Leader.
Having Gathered up his Papers, the Stout Stranger
was Preparing to Depart when, with a Cry of Annoy-
ance, he Discovered that he had Left his Purse on the
What-Not in his Office. Did the Industrious Youth
Happen to have Five Guineas Upon him? It was
Vital that Sir John should be Retained forthwith, as

the Other Side might Snap him Up. The Industrious Youth was Afraid he had Only Got Three Pounds, but the Stout Stranger was Very Nice about it and said he Could Probably Borrow the Balance from Sir John's Clerk. The Stout Stranger then Withdrew, Leaving behind him a Fragrant Smell of Cloves. As the Expected Instructions did not Come, the Industrious Youth Caused Enquiries to be Made at Sir John's Chambers. But Sir John's Clerk had not Seen or Heard of the Stout Stranger. And as the Instructions have not Yet arrived the Industrious Youth is of Opinion that the Stout Stranger must have Met with a Serious Accident, or been Visited by a Sudden and Complete Loss of Memory.

Moral.—*Caveat Junior.*

MR. WHITEWIG AND THE RASH
QUESTION

MR. WHITEWIG AND THE RASH
QUESTION

∾

M R. WHITEWIG was Greatly Gratified when
the Judge of Assize Invited him to Defend a
Prisoner who was Charged with Having
Stolen a Pair of Boots, a Mouse-Trap, and Fifteen
Packets of Gold Flakes. It was his First Case and he
Meant to Make a Good Show. Mr. Whitewig
Studied the Depositions Carefully and Came to the
Conclusion that a Skilful Cross-Examination of the
Witnesses and a Tactful Speech would Secure the
Acquittal of the Accused. When the Prisoner (an
Ill-Looking Person) was Placed in the Dock, Mr.
Whitewig Approached that Receptacle and Informed
the Prisoner that he Might, if he Wished, Give
Evidence on Oath. From the Prisoner's Reply (in
which he Alluded to Grandmothers and Eggs) Mr.
Whitewig Gathered that he did not Propose to Avail
Himself of this Privilege. The Case Began. At
First All Went Well. The Prosecutor Admitted to
Mr. Whitewig that he Could not be Sure that the
Man he had Seen Lurking in the Neighbourhood of
his Emporium was the Prisoner; and the Prosecutor's
Assistant Completely Failed to Identify the Boots, the
Mouse-Trap, or the Gold Flakes by Pointing to any
Distinctive Peculiarities which they Exhibited. By
the Time the Police Inspector Entered the Witness-
Box Mr. Whitewig Felt that the Case was Won. Mr.

Whitewig Cunningly Extracted from the Inspector the Fact that the Prisoner had Joined Up in 1914, and that the Prisoner's Wife was Expecting an Addition to her Family. He was about to Sit Down when a Final Question Occurred to him. "Having Regard to this Man's Record," he Sternly Asked, "How Came You to Arrest him?" The Inspector Drew a Bundle of Blue Documents from the Recesses of his Uniform, and, Moistening his Thumb, Read therefrom. Mr. Whitewig Learned in Silent Horror that the Prisoner's Record Included Nine Previous Convictions. When the Prisoner was Asked whether he had Anything to say why Sentence should not be Passed Upon him, he Said some Very Disagreeable Things about the Mug who had Defended him.

Moral.—*Leave Well Alone.*

THE K.C., M.P., AND THE BILL FOR THE
SUPPRESSION OF NIGHT CLUBS

THE K.C., M.P., AND THE BILL FOR
THE
SUPPRESSION OF NIGHT CLUBS

∽

A DISTINGUISHED K.C., M.P., having Balloted Successfully, became Entitled to Introduce a Bill Under the Ten Minutes' Rule. He Decided in Favour of a Bill for the Suppression of Night Clubs. The K.C., M.P., was a Man of Blameless Life and Old-Fashioned Views. Of Night Clubs he had no Personal Experience, and he Felt that he Ought to See for himself the Evils which he Desired to Stamp Out. Disguised in a Curly Wig and a Moustache (which he Secured in Covent Garden) he Repaired on Monday to the "Giddy Goat." His Worst Expectations were Realised. On Tuesday he Tried the "Bubble and Squeak," where he was Greatly Surprised and Distressed. On Wednesday he Obtained Admission to the "Tiddlywinks" and Got Home at Four A.M. On Thursday he Tried the "Giddy Goat" again. On Friday he Took Some Dancing Lessons from Madame Frou-Frou in Shaftesbury Avenue. On Saturday he became a Life Member of "Pongo's." At the Latter Establishment he Found a Lady Member who Told him that he Danced Awfully Sweetly, and they Had Supper Together. The Bill (Including Eight *Crème-de-Menthes* and Two Bottles of *Veuve Monte Cristo*) Came to Nine Pounds Eleven Shillings and Nine Pence. During the Raid which Occurred in the Small Hours of the Morning the K.C., M.P., Mingled with the Orchestra and was Able to Satisfy the Police that he was a Professional Player of the Ukulele. Thinking Matters Over during the Week-End he Came to the Conclusion that the Case against Night Clubs had been Greatly Exaggerated. The K.C., M.P., therefore Scrapped his Projected Measure, and Substituted a Bill for the Further Amendment of the Law of Property Act, 1925.

Moral.—*Experientia Docet.*

MR. JUSTICE CATTEMALL AND
MR. JUSTICE DEARLOVE

94

MR. JUSTICE CATTEMALL AND
MR. JUSTICE DEARLOVE

∾

MR. JUSTICE CATTEMALL and Mr. Justice Dearlove were Experienced Judges of the King's Bench Division. Their Views and Methods in Connection with the Treatment of Prisoners Differed Widely. Cattemall, J., always Looked in *Archbold's Criminal Pleading* to See How Much he could Give them, and Proceeded to Give it. If there were Three Counts in the Indictment he Ladled out Five Years on each Count, and Made them Run Consecutively. The Lamentations of the Relatives of the Accused Seemed Rather to Gratify him than Otherwise. When he Went on Circuit the Home Office Laid on an Extra Temporary Staff to Deal with the Petitions which Poured in; and the Court of Criminal Appeal Became so Busy that it had to Borrow a Judge from the Admiralty Division to Cope with the Work. Mr. Justice Dearlove was the Very Opposite of his Learned Brother. He Liked to Bind Over the Wicked to Come up for Judgment if Called Upon, and he Shed Tears when he had to Send Anyone to Prison. Towards Old Offenders he was Particularly Gentle, because they had Never had a Chance; and he Let Off all Youthful Malefactors because he did not Wish to make Criminals of them. Cattemall, J., and Dearlove, J., often Discussed the Relative Merits of their Respective Systems. Here is a Picture of them so Discussing. The Short One is Cattemall, J., and the Tall One is Dearlove, J.

Moral.—*You Never Can Tell.*

THE SOUND LAWYER WHO MADE
A GOOD RESOLUTION

THE SOUND LAWYER WHO MADE
A GOOD RESOLUTION

ᛞ

THERE was Once a Sound Lawyer who was Firmly Resolved that if he should ever Receive Judicial Honours he would Avoid the Errors and Failings of Some of his Predecessors. In Particular he would not Indulge in Foolish Jokes, Give Vent to Irrelevant Observations about Men and Things, or Hint that the Bar had Sadly Deteriorated Since he had Ceased to Adorn its Ranks. In Due Course the Sound Lawyer (Whose Brother-in-Law was a Personage of Some Importance) was Invited by the Authorities to Accept a County Court Judgeship. By Return of Post the Sound Lawyer Intimated that he was Ready and Willing to Grapple With the Job. Grimly Determined to Adhere to his Good Resolution, he Took his Seat on the Bench. Did he Adhere to his Good Resolution? He did not. Before the Year was Out the Reporters in his Court had Recorded that a Plymouth Brother could not be Believed upon his Oath; that it was Common Knowledge that a Married Woman was either a Slave or a Tyrant; that while at the Bar the Sound Lawyer had Frequently been so Overworked that he had not been in Bed for a Week; that the Moral Standards of Artists and Literary Men were Extremely Low; that the Legislators of the County were Obviously Half-Witted; and that Anybody who Read Boccacio could

97

Understand why the Latin Races were so Greatly Inferior to the Inhabitants of These Islands. They had also Taken Down a Variety of Time-honoured Jests Turning upon the Thrifty Habits of Scotchmen and the Irritating Ways of Mothers-in-Law. And the Sound Lawyer had so often Cited Apposite Extracts from the Works of Cicero, Ben Jonson, Rabelais, Tennyson, and Other Authors, both Ancient and Modern, that in Order to Get them Down Correctly each of the Reporters had been Compelled to Purchase a Copy of the "Book of Quotations," in which the Sound Lawyer Discovered them.

Moral.—*Make Good Resolutions.*

THE KINDLY JUDGE AND THE
LADY BARRISTER

THE KINDLY JUDGE AND THE
LADY BARRISTER

∽

A LEARNED JUDGE, on Arriving at the
Royal Courts of Justice to Deal with the
Non-Jury List, was Told by his Clerk that one
of the Counsel in the First Case was Miss Mary
Poppleton, the Newly-Called Lady Barrister. The
Judge, who was Kindly, Large-Minded, and an
Upholder of the Cause of Woman, Determined that
he would Give Miss Mary Poppleton a Good Run.
When the Judge took his Seat he Felt that the Fragile
Creature with a Squeaky Voice and a Mild Blue Eye
who Appeared for the Plaintiff would Need all his
Help. For a Robust and Fierce-Looking Individual
was Representing the Defendant.

The Case Began. Whenever he had a Chance the
Judge gave the Mild Blue Eye a Leg-Up. And he
Made a Point of Treating the Fierce-Looking Advo-
cate on the Other Side with Some Severity. Ulti-
mately (though not without Misgiving) the Judge
Gave Judgment for the Mild Blue Eye with Costs.
The Fierce-Looking Opponent, who had Cross-
Examined with Effect and Delivered a Pointed Legal
Argument, Promptly Asked for a Stay of Execution.

When the Court Adjourned the Judge's Clerk
Expressed the View that he had been Rather Hard on
Miss Mary Poppleton. The Judge angrily Enquired
what the Clerk Meant, and Learned, Too Late, that

he had been Misled by Appearances. It seemed that the Mild Blue Eye was a Young Man who had Steered the University Eight to Victory Three Years Ago, and that the Fierce-Looking Counsel for the Defendant was Miss Mary Poppleton. But Happily no Harm was Done. For Miss Mary Poppleton Promptly Went to the Court of Appeal and had an Easy Win.

Moral.—*Spot the Lady*.

THE EXPERIENCED ADVOCATE AND THE
HALF-YEAR'S RENT

THE EXPERIENCED ADVOCATE AND
THE HALF-YEAR'S RENT

∽

AN Experienced Advocate Left the Royal Courts
of Justice in a Happy Frame of Mind after a
Full and Satisfactory Day. He had Won the
First Case by Pointing Out to the Jury that the
Principal Witness for the Enemy had Professed to
Remember Details which Must (had his Story been
True) have Passed from his Mind. His Second Vic-
tory was Due to his Reminder of the Jury that the
Plaintiff had failed to Recall Incidents which Must
(had his Account of the Matter in Question been
Honest) have Dwelt in his Memory. His Third
Triumph was the Result of a Successful Invitation to
the Jury to Say that a City Merchant who Pretended
that he had Forgotten to Fill Up the Counterfoil of an
Important Cheque Ought not to be—Nay, Could not
be—Believed upon his Oath. He was Pleased with
himself. On Returning to Chambers the Experienced Advocate Found on his Desk a Peremptory
Reminder that his Half-Year's Rent was Due and
Owing. The Experienced Advocate was Indignant
because he Felt Sure he had Already Sent a Cheque
for the Amount. He Distinctly Remembered Blot-
ting the Date of the Cheque and Filling up the
Counterfoil. The Experienced Advocate, having
Examined his Pass-Book and Cheque-Book, Ascertained that during the Past Twelve Months he had not

Filled up any Counterfoils at all, and, furthermore, that he had not Sent a Cheque, whether Blotted or Otherwise, for the Half-Year's Rent. The Experienced Advocate Rejoiced More than Ever Over his Good Day's Work.

Moral.—*Circumstances Alter Cases.*

THE OLD STAGER AND THE EXCHEQUER SUIT

THE OLD STAGER AND THE EXCHEQUER SUIT ON THE INFORMATION OF THE ATTORNEY-GENERAL ISSUING OUT OF THE PETTY-BAG

～

ONE day an Agitated Solicitor Waited upon an Old Stager. The Latter was Replete with such Learning as is to be found in the Third Edition of "Bullen & Leake." The Agitated Solicitor Wanted the Old Stager to Advise him. There was a Firm of High Standing which Owed his Clients a Lot of Money. Though the Firm of High Standing had not a Leg to Stand upon, Order Fourteen was No Good, as they could Easily Put Up some Rotten Sort of Defence. His Clients must Have the Money Forthwith as they were in a Wobbly Financial Condition. What was he to Do?

The Old Stager Said it was Clearly a Case for an Exchequer Suit on the Information of the Attorney-General Issuing out of the Petty-Bag. He Promised to Prepare without Delay the Necessary Formal Documents. When the Agitated Solicitor had Withdrawn the Old Stager got to Work on the Draft. It Began with the Observation, "*Oyez, Oyez, Oyez,*" and Recited that the Right Honourable the Attorney-General had been Informed by his Trusty and Well-beloved Thomas Binks and Thomas Binks the younger (Trading as Binks and Company) that the Firm of High

Standing Owed them the Sum of 3,921*l.* 4*s.* 8*d.*   It Proceeded to Warn the Firm of High Standing that by Declining to pay the said Moneys they had Rendered themselves Liable to the Pains and Penalties Made and Provided by 1 & 2 Ric. II. c. 4, 18 Eliz. c. 14, and Divers Acts Amending the Same, the Provisions whereof were Preserved and Maintained by and Incorporated in the Judicature Acts of 1873 and 1875 (36 & 37 Vict. c. 66 and 38 & 39 Vict. c. 77).   It then Summoned Each and Every of the Members of the Firm of High Standing to Attend at Twelve O'Clock (Midday) on Monday (*Die Lunae*) next after the Morrow of All Souls at the Bar of the House of Lords and there Show Cause in Person why they should not be Committed to the Clock-Tower of his Majesty's Palace of Westminster or to his Majesty's Keep or Tower of London and there be Imprisoned until Further Order. In a Few Closing Sentences it Pointed Out that if they Desired to be Assoilzied, Purged, and Acquitted of the said Debt and Relieved from the Obligation of Attending at the said Bar of the said House of Lords, the Firm of High Standing must Cause the said Sum of 3,921*l.* 4*s.* 8*d.* to be Paid in Cash to the said Thomas Binks and Thomas Binks the Younger (Trading as Binks & Company) within Twenty-four Hours. At the End of the Draft the Old Stager Added the Devout Aspiration, "God Save the King."   He also Penned in the Margin a Note to the Effect that this Imposing Document should be Engrossed on Parchment and Served upon the Defendants by a Mounted Policeman. The Firm of High Standing (who were Hoping for a Government

Contract in the Near Future) were so Terrified by the Old Stager's Screed that, Without Consulting Their Solicitors, they Cashed Up At Once. When the Agitated Solicitor Subsequently Enquired of the Old Stager where he had Unearthed this Most Satisfactory Procedure, the Old Stager Modestly Confessed that he had Invented it.

Moral.—*Try it on.*

THE PRUDENT COUNSEL, THE NEW CLIENT,
AND THE STRIDENT PERSON

THE PRUDENT COUNSEL, THE NEW
CLIENT, AND THE STRIDENT PERSON

∽

THERE was once a Prudent Counsel who Took no Risks. He was Briefed for the Defendant by a New Client in a Ticklish Case. After Mature Thought the Prudent Counsel Came to the Conclusion that the Best Thing would be to Sit Tight. The Prudent Counsel Found himself Opposed by a Strident Person of Violent and Aggressive Methods. The Strident Person Made an Offensive Opening Speech, Got up a Quite Unnecessary Row with the Judge, Grossly Insulted the Prudent Counsel, and Forgot to Ask the Plaintiff the Only Important Question. The Prudent Counsel Secured Judgment without Calling the Defendant. He Felt that the New Client was his for All Time. Was the New Client Surprised and Delighted by the Performance of the Prudent Counsel? He was not. The New Client Rebuked the Prudent Counsel for his Want of Go, Dwelt upon the Admirable Fight which the Strident Person had Put Up, and thereafter Transferred to the Strident Person his Affections and all his Briefs.

Moral.—*Raise Your Voice.*

THE TEARFUL PERFORMER AND THE
PLAINTIFF WITH A PAST

THE TEARFUL PERFORMER AND THE
PLAINTIFF WITH A PAST

∽

THERE was Once a Tearful Performer in the King's Bench Division. He Knew All the Tricks of the Trade, but his Real Strong Point was the Sob-Stuff. He Often Appeared for Plaintiffs. First he would Give the Jury a Simple Outline of the Facts. Then he Assured them that he had no Wish to Work upon Their Feelings. Later, in a More Cooing Tone of Voice, he Reluctantly Went into the Harrowing Details. By the Time he Got to the Blasted Reputation, the Shocking Injuries, or the Agony of Mind (as the Case might be), there was not a Dry Handkerchief in Court. So Formidable was his Advocacy that Insurance Companies and Newspapers Usually Settled Up on Hearing that the Tearful Performer had been retained. One Fine Day, when his Engagements were Many, the Tearful Performer Rushed into Court Just in Time to Make the Final Speech for the Plaintiff in an Accident Case. He had not Heard Any of the Evidence, and his Agitated Junior only had Time to Inform him that the Plaintiff had Admitted in Cross-Examination a Conviction for Perjury at the Old Bailey Some Years Ago. The Tearful Performer was Undisturbed. He Begged the Jury not to allow themselves to be Misled by any Red Herring which his Learned Friend might Seek to Draw across the Track. He Reminded them that the

Question was whether the Defendant's Driver had been Negligent, and not whether the Plaintiff's Evidence on Another and a Different Occasion had, or had not, been Accepted. The Tearful Performer then Asked the Jury what they Thought of a Case which had to be Bolstered up by Deplorable Irrelevancies, and Invited them to Say that it was a Cruel Thing to Drag Out of a Crippled Man a Story which Must have Caused the Utmost Pain and Distress to his Innocent Wife and Children. And (Praying the Conviction in Aid) the Tearful Performer Enquired what was Better Calculated to Make a Man Absolutely Accurate in the Witness-Box for All Time than a Sentence of Imprisonment for Perjury. By the Time he had Got to the Bit about Praying the Conviction in Aid, the Tearful Performer was so Choked with Emotion that he could Hardly Proceed with his Address. And as at that Moment his Clerk Told him he was Wanted in Another Court he Left the Matter there. Was the Speech of the Tearful Performer a Success? It was. The Jury Gave the Plaintiff such Enormous Damages that the Tearful Performer Advised him to Accept Half the Amount rather than Run the Risk of a New Trial being Ordered.

Moral.—*Tears bring relief.*

MR. SLASHER, MR. JUSTICE FOOZLE, AND
THE HALVED SEVENTEENTH

MR. SLASHER, MR. JUSTICE FOOZLE,
AND THE HALVED SEVENTEENTH

∽

MR. SLASHER, of Plum Tree Court, was a Promising Advocate and an Admirable Golfer. His Handicap was Four. Mr. Justice Foozle, though a Profound Lawyer, was an Indifferent Performer at the Royal and Ancient Game. He had Taken to Athletics Late in Life. His Handicap of Twenty-Four Seldom Enabled him to Secure a Victory. One Easter at the Annual Bench and Bar Tournament, Mr. Slasher Found himself Drawn as the Opponent of Foozle, J. The Committee, he was Informed, Considered that he Ought to Concede to the Learned Judge a Stroke a Hole. Mr. Slasher was Undismayed by the Burden so Put upon him. Indeed, he Backed himself to Win, Laying as Much as Three to One with Various Learned Friends. The Day of the Contest Arrived. Mr. Slasher, being a Tactful Person, Held himself in Reserve. He Permitted Mr. Justice Foozle to Win Eight of the first Sixteen Holes, Confident that he could Get the Seventeenth and Eighteenth on his Head. Thus he would Inflict on Foozle, J., a Defeat which Carried with it no Humiliation. But at the Short Seventeenth an Unexpected Event Occurred. Foozle, J., was on the Extreme Edge of the Green with his Third. Mr. Slasher, as the Result of a Beautiful Iron Shot, Laid his Ball Dead with his Second. As the

Learned Judge's Ball was a Good Three Yards from the Pin it was Clear that only a Miracle could Save him. After Examining the Position Closely, Mr. Justice Foozle, with a Look of Extreme Innocence, Uttered the Word "Halved" and Picked up his Ball. Mr. Slasher was so Taken Aback by the Tactics of Foozle, J., that he Topped his Drive to the Eighteenth, Sliced into the Rough with his Second, Was out of Bounds with his Third, and Ultimately was Down in Nine. Whereas Mr. Justice Foozle, Greatly Heartened by the Halved Seventeenth, Did a Magnificent Five and Won the Match. The Result of it all was that Mr. Slasher Lost Twenty Odd Pounds that he could Ill Afford. Did Foozle, J., Exhibit Any Remorse? None whatever. And when Mr. Slasher next Appeared in Judge's Chambers, Mr. Justice Foozle Addressed him as "Mr. Tompkins," and Ordered him to Pay the Costs in Any Event.

Moral.—*Play Up.*

THE MATURE JUNIOR AND THE
DILIGENT PUPIL

THE MATURE JUNIOR AND THE
DILIGENT PUPIL

ᔆ

A MATURE Junior had a Diligent Pupil who
Wanted to Know All about Everything. So
Insatiable was his Thirst for Knowledge that
the Patience of the Mature Junior was Sorely Tried.
From Morning till Night the Diligent Pupil Plied
him with Questions about Practice and Procedure,
Professional Etiquette, Case-Law and Legal Biography till his Head Span. The Time Came when
the Mature Junior Felt he Could not Stand It Much
Longer. One Fine Day the Mature Junior was Unex-
pectedly Deserted by his Leader at a Critical Moment.
The Case had Taken a Nasty Turn and the Leader
Suddenly Remembered that he had to Send a Tele-
gram. The Diligent Pupil (who was Sitting Behind
the Mature Junior) Asked him whether the Leader
would Soon Come Back, and Expressed the View
that the Judge Seemed to be Rather Against them.
He also Begged to be Told the Name of the Leader on
the Other Side. When the Mature Junior was about
to Address the Jury the Diligent Pupil Wanted to
Know why the Judge was Wearing Violet Robes.
He Thought the Mature Junior had Told him they
were Never Worn in Jury Cases. The Case was
Part Heard when the Court Rose and the Mature
Junior was Feeling Distinctly Irritable. In Particular he was Worried about his Engagements for the

Following Day. As Soon as he Got Back to his Chambers the Diligent Pupil Asked him when his Case would be Reached in the Court of Appeal, what he Would Do if it Came on before the Part-Heard Case was Finished, and Whether the Diligent Pupil could Join more than one Circuit. The Mature Junior Saw Red, and Struck the Diligent Pupil a Heavy Blow with a Blunt Instrument, to wit, the Poker. When the Diligent Pupil had Recovered Consciousness the Mature Junior Ordered him, on Pain of Death, never to Reappear in his Chambers.

Moral.—*Suffer Pupils Gladly*.

THE JUNIOR WHO LUNCHED AT THE CLUB,
THE BALD OLD GENTLEMAN, AND
THE HEAVY BRIEF

THE JUNIOR WHO LUNCHED AT THE CLUB, THE BALD OLD GENTLEMAN, AND THE HEAVY BRIEF

∽

A JUNIOR sat in his Chambers after Lunching at the Club. There was a Good Fire, and the Arm-Chair was Comfortable. Suddenly a Bald Old Gentleman of Dignified Appearance Stood before him. He Carried a Black Bag. Having Wished the Junior a Good Afternoon he Observed that he was Leaving a Brief for him, and that he would Like to Tell him Something about the Case. It was a Big Affair in the Commercial Court, and there would be Three Leaders who had all Pledged their Word to be Present throughout the Hearing. "You will have," the Bald Old Gentleman Proceeded, "another Junior with you. He has already Settled the Pleadings." "The Case," he Proceeded, "must Last for at Least Three Weeks, and it is bound to Go to the Court of Appeal and the House of Lords. And when the Questions of Principle have been Decided there will be Further Heavy Litigation here-after." The Bald Old Gentleman then Drew Out his Fountain-Pen and a Cheque-Book, and Said that the Clients Wished that all the Brief-Fees should be Paid forthwith. Just as he was Asking the Junior whether he could Tell him what was Two-Thirds of Two Thousand Five Hundred Guineas, the Clerk Crashed into the Room and Woke the Junior up.

The Clerk Wished to Remind the Junior that the Petty-Cash was Exhausted, and that if he Wanted to be in Time for the County Court Case To-morrow Morning he would have to Catch the Eight Twenty-Two at Fenchurch Street. The Junior Swore Horribly and, Composing himself once more to Slumber, Sought to Recapture this Delicious Dream.

Moral.—*Dormientibus Felicitas Venit.*

BEEFY THOMAS AND ANÆMIC HENRY

BEEFY THOMAS AND ANÆMIC HENRY

∽

THOMAS and Henry were Barristers-at-Law who Shared Chambers in the Temple. Thomas was of Beefy Build but Mediocre Intelligence. Henry was an Anæmic and Brainy Person of Insignificant Appearance. When the European War Broke Out, Anæmic Henry and Beefy Thomas, being of Military Age, Determined to Do their Bit. Anæmic Henry Joined Up, and Proceeded to Flanders, Gallipoli, and Mesopotamia, where he was Gassed, Shelled, Machine-Gunned, Frozen, and Baked during the Ensuing Three Years. Beefy Thomas was Less Precipitate. He Stayed at Home and Made Recruiting Speeches, which were so Manly and Eloquent that Hundreds Flocked to the Colours. The Authorities Soon Rewarded him with the Position of Legal Adviser to the Margarine and Fatty Extracts Ministry. As Legal Adviser, Beefy Thomas Exhibited Great Industry in Drafting Orders-in-Council. After an Unsuccessful Endeavour to Explain to a Law-Officer the Meaning of Margarine Order No. 643, his Further Promotion was Decided upon. Beefy Thomas Became Deputy-Assistant-Supervisor of the Naval and Military Stores (Detraining and Dispatch) Department, with the Temporary Rank of Brigadier-General, and Went to France. For Two Years he Discharged his Duties at Boulogne-Sur-Mer with Quiet Efficiency. He Looked Very Fine in his

Uniform and Decorations. On One Occasion he had the Pleasure of Doing Anæmic Henry a Service. Anæmic Henry was Returning to the Front, and Beefy Thomas Found him an Empty Cattle-Truck to Travel in. When the War Came to an End Beefy Thomas Stood for Parliament. He Got in on his Head. Anæmic Henry went Back to the Temple in a C.3 State of Health. He Found that his Clients had Forgotten him. But Happily the Influence of Beefy Thomas was able to Secure for Anæmic Henry the Attorney-Generalship of the Lower Cannibal Islands, and if Anæmic Henry Can Stand the Climate he will Become Chief Justice in Due Course.

Moral.—*Be Brave*.

YOUNG MR. TITTLEBAT, THE LEADING
SOLICITOR, AND THE UNEXPECTED
VICTORY

YOUNG MR. TITTLEBAT, THE LEADING SOLICITOR, AND THE UNEXPECTED VICTORY

∽

YOUNG Mr. Tittlebat was Visited One Evening in his Chambers by a Leading Solicitor. He Wanted Mr. Tittlebat to Take a Brief in a Case which was to be Heard the Next Day. But as the Defendant (for whom Mr. Tittlebat was to Appear) had no Defence, would Mr. Tittlebat Accept a Fee of One Guinea? Mr. Tittlebat, who had Hitherto been Unemployed, Gladly Assented to this Proposal. On Perusing the Papers Mr. Tittlebat (who was not without Intelligence) Detected a Flaw in the Plaintiff's Armour. And, Sure Enough, on the Morrow Mr. Tittlebat Obtained Judgment, with Costs, for the Astonished Defendant. When the Case was Over there was a Scene of Great Enthusiasm in the Corridor, and both the Defendant and the Leading Solicitor Insisted upon Entertaining Mr. Tittlebat at Luncheon. The Leading Solicitor Asked Mr. Tittlebat which Circuit he Went, and whether he had Any Objection to Parliamentary Work. And he Twice took a Note of Mr. Tittlebat's Temple Address. At a Late Hour Mr. Tittlebat Returned to Chambers, Flushed with Victory and Refreshments, Satisfied that his Career was Made. Twenty Years Elapsed and Mr. Tittlebat, now a Bald and Prosperous Person, Received a Visit from the Leading Solicitor.

He did not Bring a Brief with him this Time, but Said he had Just Looked In to Ask Mr. Tittlebat Whether he Remembered that Glorious Victory of Twenty Years Ago. The Leading Solicitor Added that he had Often Wondered how Mr. Tittlebat was Getting On.

Moral.—*Gratitude takes Many Forms.*

THE AUSTRALIAN PLUTOCRAT,
THE MILLIONAIRE'S NEPHEW, AND
THE OLD BAILEY PRACTITIONER

THE AUSTRALIAN PLUTOCRAT, THE MILLIONAIRE'S NEPHEW, AND THE OLD BAILEY PRACTITIONER

∽

ONE Evening an Old Bailey Practitioner was Seated in the Splendid Lounge of the Cosmopolitan Hotel, Smoking an After-Dinner Cigar and Watching the Giddy Throng about him. To his Great Amusement a Gentleman with an Australian Intonation Professed to Recognise him as a Fellow-Traveller on the *Gigantic*. The Old Bailey Practitioner, Anticipating Developments, Encouraged the Stranger to Converse. It Seemed that he was a Wealthy Piano-Manufacturer from Wagga-Wagga Enjoying a Well-Earned Holiday. Before Long, Another Gentleman (with a Cork Accent) Asked whether he might Join them. He was, it Appeared, in a Great Difficulty. His Uncle, a Millionaire in Chicago, had Left him $10,000 to Distribute in Charity, and he Badly Wanted Advice as to the Legal Formalities to be Observed by those who Wished to Present Large Sums to Hospitals. He was Over-joyed to Discover that the Old Bailey Practitioner was a Lawyer; and when the Old Bailey Practitioner (more Amused than ever) Consented to Distribute 500*l*. on his behalf, the Millionaire's Nephew did not Know how to Express his Gratitude. He Said he had the 500*l*. in his Wallet and was Ready to Hand it Over Forthwith. The Australian Plutocrat then

Suggested that the Confidence which Each Reposed in the Other would be Greatly Strengthened if the Old Bailey Practitioner were to Entrust the Millionaire's Nephew with his Purse. The Old Bailey Practitioner (Hardly Able to Restrain his Laughter) said he would Gladly Do So. The Exchange was Quickly Effected and the Australian Plutocrat and the Millionaire's Nephew Declared they would be Back in a Quarter of an Hour. Before they were Fifty Yards from the Hotel the Old Bailey Practitioner had Handed them over to an Intelligent Constable on the Charge of Obtaining Money by means of the Confidence Trick. The Next Day the Old Bailey Practitioner had Two Nasty Shocks. First, the Police Informed him that the Wallet Really Contained 500*l*. Secondly, the Australian Plutocrat and the Millionaire's Nephew Loudly Protested that the Old Bailey Practitioner was the Trickster, and that he had Induced them to Take his Purse in Exchange for the Wallet. And they Pointed Out that whereas their Statement about the Wallet was perfectly True, the Cash in the Purse of the Old Bailey Practitioner Totalled Nine Shillings and Ten Pence in Silver and Bronze. The Magistrate Said that the Old Bailey Practitioner was Lucky not to be in the Dock, and Discharged the Accused. As they Left the Court they Winked in a Knowing Fashion at the Prosecutor. The Old Bailey Practitioner Bitterly Regretted his Hasty Action. It was now Clear to him that this was the Confidence Trick in a New Form. His Anguish was Increased by a Fierce Letter from an Eminent Firm Threatening an Action for Malicious Prosecution.   The End of it was that the Old Bailey Practitioner had to Pay 100*l.* to the Australian Plutocrat, the Same Amount to the Millionaire's Nephew, and 50*l.* to the Eminent Firm for their Agreed Costs.

Moral.—*Festina Lente.*

THE JUDGE OF ASSIZE AND THE
OLD SCHOOL FRIEND

THE JUDGE OF ASSIZE AND THE OLD SCHOOL FRIEND

ᔈ

A JUDGE of Assize, when his Circuit Labours were Concluded, Asked the Governor of the Prison to Show him Over his Establishment. When they Got to the Exercise Yard the Judge of Assize, rather to his Dismay, Recognised an Old School Friend. The Old School Friend had been a Financier and was now Taking the Consequences. Having Obtained Permission to do so, the Judge of Assize Addressed the Old School Friend. Assuming an Expression of Melancholy Sympathy, he Expressed a Hope that the Old School Friend was Bearing Up. The Old School Friend Assured him that he was Exceedingly Well. In Fact, he had never been so Well in his Life. He had Done Five Years, and so would be Out in a Few Months. His Future, he was Glad to Say, was Assured, as he had Taken the Precaution of Making a Handsome Settlement on his Wife before the Crash. He Hoped the Judge of Assize would Visit them at their Villa in the South of France if he Happened to be in Those Parts during the Winter. The Old School Friend then Begged to be Informed as to the Health and Happiness of the Judge of Assize. The Latter Sadly Replied that he was Gouty and Rheumatic, Overworked, and still Separated from his Pension by a Period of Nine Years. His Children, moreover, had Given him a Great Deal of Trouble and Anxiety, and he hadn't Saved a Bob. The Old School Friend said it was Too Bad, and Opined that there was a Great Deal to be said for a Financial Career.

Moral.—*There are Two Sides to Every Question.*

THE EMERITUS PROFESSOR OF INTERNATIONAL
LAW AND THE POLICE COURT BRIEF

THE EMERITUS PROFESSOR OF
INTERNATIONAL LAW AND THE
POLICE COURT BRIEF

∽

THERE was once an Emeritus Professor of International Law. His Learning was Stupendous. He was a D.C.L. and LL.D. Many Times Over. The Public Orators of Oxford, Cambridge, Durham, Sheffield, Birmingham, and Aberystwyth (to Mention only a Few) had Striven in Their Best Latin to do Justice to his Erudition when he Presented himself to Receive their Honorary Degrees. One of them Enquired "*Quae Regio Terrae Vestri Non Plena Laboris?*" Another Greeted him as "*Scientiae Pene Novae Inclytus Propugnator.*" A Third Remarked that he was "*Maxime Egregius Philosophus.*" A Fourth that he was "*Spectatissimus Doctor.*" And a Fifth, who Proclaimed him to be "*Juris Inter Omnes Nationes Observandi Peritissimus,*" was Thought to have Hit the Right Nail on the Head. Four Massive Tomes which the Emeritus Professor had Compiled Entitled "Peace and War," "the Doctrine of *Renvoi*," "The Three-Mile Limit," and "The Declaration of Paris, Its Genesis and Implications," had been Translated into French, German, Spanish, Russian, Urdu, and Chinese. The Emeritus Professor had a Considerable Beard, Large Spectacles, a Weak Voice and Flat Feet.

When he was at the Height of his Fame it

Happened that the Private Secretary of the Baratarian Ambassador, being Short of Cash, Endeavoured to Stabilise his Finances by Means of a Stumer Cheque and so Placed himself within the Grip of the Law. An Intelligent Solicitor, Hastily Summoned to the Embassy, Advised that the Emeritus Professor should be Retained At Once to Defend the Private Secretary. It was Clearly a Case, he said, in which the Privilege of Exterritoriality should be Invoked, and None but the Emeritus Professor could Deal Adequately with that Difficult Topic.

The Emeritus Professor, Duly Briefed, Proceeded to the Mulberry Street Police Court. With him he Took some Two Dozen Volumes of Text-books and Reports.

When the Emeritus Professor Seated himself in the Pen Provided for Counsel the Dock was already Occupied. The Magistrate Asked the Emeritus Professor whether he Appeared for the Accused. He Replied in the Affirmative and Began his Discourse.

The Emeritus Professor Led Off with a Few Pages of *Westlake* and *Hall*, and then, Warming to his Work, Read Several Cogent Passages, from *Grotius*, *Puffendorf*, and *Bynkershoek*. He Dwelt, in Particular, on the Second Half of Chapter XIII. ("*De Foro Legatorum*") of the last-named Authority. The Magistrate Appeared to the Emeritus Professor to be both Obtuse and Impolite. He Repeatedly Tried to Stop the Emeritus Professor's Argument, and said, More than Once, that he Could not Hear or Understand what the Emeritus Professor was Saying. After Forty-Five Minutes the Magistrate Ordered the

Emeritus Professor to Sit Down. The Emeritus Professor (who by this Time was Referring the Magistrate to Bergbohn's *Staats-Verträge Und Gesetze als Quellen des Volkerrechts*) went on Unmoved. When the Emeritus Professor at last Resumed his Seat, after Reading All the Judgments in *The "Parlement Belge,"*[1] he had been Speaking for an Hour and a Half, and the Magistrate was Foaming at the Mouth. To the Amazement of the Emeritus Professor the Magistrate Told the Defendant that he had Aggravated his Offence by Employing a Lunatic to Defend him, and Sent him to Prison for a Month. It was not till the Next Day that the Emeritus Professor Realised that he had Gone to the Wrong Police Court and that the Defendant on whose Behalf he had Delivered his Oration was an Italian Costermonger who had Obstructed the Traffic with his Barrow and Assaulted the Police.

Moral.—*Choose Your Tribunal Wisely.*

[1] 4 P.D. 129; 5 P.D. 197.

MR. FLEDGLING AND THE APPLICATION FOR
PARTICULARS OF THE STATEMENT OF CLAIM

MR. FLEDGLING AND THE APPLICATION
FOR PARTICULARS OF THE STATEMENT
OF CLAIM

∽

MR. FLEDGLING was Filled with Wild Elation when his First Job Turned Up. It was a Summons in the King's Bench Division. He was to Appear at One-Thirty before a Master of the Supreme Court of Judicature and Apply for Particulars of the Statement of Claim. With regard to Paragraph 1 he was to Insist upon Precise Information as to whether the Alleged Agreement was Oral or in Writing, and, if the Latter, as to the Document or Documents Purporting to Contain it. So far as Paragraph 3 was Concerned, he was to Press for Further Details as to the Alleged Defects in the Said Goods. And the Vagueness of Paragraph 4, he Gathered, Necessitated a Closer Definition of the Loss and Damage Alleged to have been Suffered by the Plaintiff. Two Sleepless Nights were Succeeded by Two Days of Anxious Research, and on the Third Day Mr. Fledgling Tottered to the Field of Battle, Carrying his Books of Reference in a Blue Bag. He Arrived in the Bear-Garden to Find his Elderly Opponent already on the Spot. Mr. Fledgling Noted with Satisfaction that the Elderly Opponent Seemed to be Troubled at the Sight of his Authorities. Whilst Waiting for the Door of the Master's Room to be Flung Open Mr. Fledgling Quietly Went over the

Heads of his Arguments. He was Glad to Find that he was Quite Calm. At last the Dread Moment Arrived and Mr. Fledgling was Standing before the Master with his Elderly Opponent at his Side. The Elderly Opponent said "Good Morning, Master," in a Somewhat Familiar Fashion, but the Master, though rather Formidable in Appearance, did not Appear to Mind. While Mr. Fledgling was Explaining to the Master in a Shaky Voice the Terms of the Order and Rule under which the Application was being Made, the Elderly Opponent said he was Quite Ready to give the Particulars. The Master Observed "All Right" and Wrote a Few Words in a Deplorable Hand on the Summons. Mr. Fledgling Could hardly Believe his Ears. He had Won, Hands Down. When he Got Home that Evening Mr. Fledgling Told his People all about it. They Gathered that Mr. Fledgling had Gone Through a Trying Ordeal; that it had been a Ding-Dong Thing; and that, but for the Grim Determination of Mr. Fledgling and his Refusal to be Browbeaten by the Master or his Elderly Opponent, the Day would have been Lost.

Moral.—*Be Thorough.*

THE PROUD PARENT WHO DID HIS
BEST FOR ALFRED

THE PROUD PARENT WHO DID HIS
BEST FOR ALFRED

A PROUD PARENT was Determined that his Son Alfred should Succeed at the Bar. He therefore Consulted the Wisest of his Friends upon the All-important Question of how Alfred should be Trained to this End. They All Advised him Fully. And the Proud Parent Followed their Advice. Alfred Began by Doing three Trips on a Tramp Steamer in the Mediterranean; then he Went to Learn Colloquial French in the Cathedral City of Tours (because the Touraine Accent is so Perfect); and thereafter he Acquired Conversational German at Bonn (where the University Discipline is so Helpful to the Young). Alfred next Proceeded to Pick Up Business Methods in a Big Commercial House. Four Years having thus Sped by, Alfred did Twelve Months with a City Solicitor, a Second Twelve Months in the Chambers of a Conveyancer in Lincoln's Inn, and a Third Twelve Months in those of a Stuff-gownsman in the Temple. All would, no doubt, have been Well with Alfred's Career at the Bar had he been Able to Get Through the Examination in Roman Law. But, despite the Persistent Efforts of the Most Accomplished Coaches, he could not Perform this Feat. Driven to Select an Alternative Occupation for Alfred, the Proud Parent Answered a Number of Advertisements in the Public Journals; and Alfred is now in Charge of a Chicken Farm near Eye, in the County of Suffolk, where he also Breeds Angora Rabbits.

Moral.—*Consult Your Friends.*

THE IDLE APPRENTICE AND THE
INDUSTRIOUS DITTO

THE IDLE APPRENTICE AND THE
INDUSTRIOUS DITTO

ॐ

TWO Apprentices to the Law Shared Chambers together. The One was Idle; the Other was Industrious. The Latter Rose Early, Abstained from Strong Drink and Tobacco, Read the Law Reports, Attended Debating Societies, and Held Briefs for his Learned Friends. The Former Stayed in Bed till Mid-day, Arrived at Chambers at One, Lunched from Two to Four, Borrowed Sums of Money from his Acquaintances, Consumed Considerable Quantities of Alcohol between his Abundant Meals, and Devoted his Spare Time to Studying the Sporting Papers and Spotting Winners. The Industrious Apprentice was Ultimately Rewarded for his Virtuous Conduct. After Twenty-Three Years of Unrequited Toil, he Attracted the Favourable Notice of a Silk, who Gave him a Room and a Hundred a Year for Noting his Briefs. Far Different was the Fate of the Idle Apprentice. He Made Friends with a Moneyed Person, Got into Polite Society, Married a Charming Wife, and is now the Managing Director of the Amalgamated Continental & Asiatic Tea, Rubber, Tin & Indigo Syndicate, Limited, with an Annual Salary of Twelve Thousand Pounds.

Moral.—*Work Hard.*

THE YOUNG SOLICITOR AND THE
SAGACIOUS OLD BUFFER

THE YOUNG SOLICITOR AND THE
SAGACIOUS OLD BUFFER

∽

THERE was Once a Young Solicitor who Began to Fear that he would Never Get On. He Worked Hard, but, Try as he Might, he Could not Learn any Law. Persons who Sought his Advice were Clearly Disappointed when the Young Solicitor Told them he would Look it Up and Let Them Know To-morrow. The Young Solicitor therefore Determined to Consult a Sagacious Old Buffer whose Name was a Household Word in the Profession. The Street in which the Old Buffer's Palatial Offices were Situate was Blocked from Morning to Night by the Rolls-Royces of the Bankers, Ladies in Distress, Shipowners, Jockeys, and Dignitaries of the Church who Desired his Assistance. The Old Buffer Made them Pay through the Nose, but they all Went Away Satisfied that they had Received Good Value for their Money. Nor was this Surprising. For the Old Buffer Possessed both a Dignified Appearance and a Sympathetic Manner, and was Never at a Loss when a Complicated Legal Problem had to be Solved. The Old Buffer Always Remembered that Baron Parke, or Cairns, or Blackburn had Discussed the Topic in an Old Case. He would then Tell his Clerk to Bring him "2 Meeson & Welsby," "6 Term Reports," or "4 Barnewall & Cresswell";

and, Lo and Behold, the Volume was Sure to Contain Something Apposite and Helpful. When the Client Expressed his Astonishment at the Old Buffer's Amazing Feat of Memory he would Smile Quietly and Say it was Nothing. The Old Buffer Received the Young Solicitor with the Utmost Courtesy and Listened Attentively to his Story. When he had Finished, the Old Buffer Locked the Door and Whispered to the Young Solicitor that, if he would Swear Never to Divulge it to a Soul, he would Impart to him the Secret of his Success. "Like you," said the Old Buffer, with Tears in his Eyes, "I Knew no Law and Could not Learn any of the Beastly Stuff. But One Day I found on a Railway Book-Stall an Admirable Work Entitled 'Law for the Million.' It Cost Two Shillings and Six Pence. I Saw at once that it was a Mine of Useful Information. I Purchased Three Copies and had them Rebound. One is Called '2 Meeson & Welsby,' Another is '6 Term Reports,' and the Third is '4 Barnewell & Cresswell." When I am Asked to Advise about a Charter Party, a Bill of Sale, a Gambling Debt, or a Faculty I Turn Up the Appropriate Heading with the Happiest Results. I Strongly Advise You to Do the Same. The Book is Arranged Alphabetically," the Old Buffer Concluded, "so that it is Quite Easy to Find what you Want."

The Young Solicitor Thanked the Old Buffer Warmly and Withdrew.

Within Five Years the Young Solicitor was a Knight, a Member of Parliament, the Owner of Three Cars, and a Resident in Carlton House Terrace. And if the Old Buffer had not Retired from Practice meanwhile (with a Cool Quarter of a Million) the Young Solicitor would Assuredly have Cut him Out.

Moral.—*Bind Your Books Carefully.*

THE JUDGE WHOSE APPEARANCE
TERRIFIED THE PUBLIC

THE JUDGE WHOSE APPEARANCE
TERRIFIED THE PUBLIC

∽

ON the Opening Day of the Michaelmas Sittings no Figure in the Judicial Procession was More Awe-Inspiring than that of Mr. Justice Mildew. His Lordship's Grim Countenance Struck Terror into All Beholders. As he Walked up the Central Hall of the Royal Courts of Justice, Barristers, Managing Clerks, Office-Boys, and Flappers Shook in their Shoes and Thanked their Stars they were not Standing before him in the Dock. It was Clear to All of them that Mr. Justice Mildew had Something of Grave Importance on his Mind, and that he was Thinking Deeply. They were Right. Mr. Justice Mildew was Reflecting, as the Procession Started, that the Champagne at the Lord Chancellor's Breakfast was (for a Light Wine) Uncommonly Good, that it was a Pity he had not Taken a Third Glass, and that he had Better Find Out Where it Came From before he went Circuit. Half-way up the Hall, Mr. Justice Mildew was Wondering whether the Port at Forty-Two Shillings (of which a Considerable Quantity had been Left Over from the Last Circuit) would be Good Enough for the Bar when they Came to Dinner, and was Sincerely Hoping that his Brother Judge would be a Bit more Lively than his Colleague at the Recent Assizes. And during the last Five Yards, when his Expression became Particularly

163

Fierce, Mr. Justice Mildew was Internally Debating whether he should Purchase a "Wilfred" or a "Gollywog" for his Youngest Grand-Daughter, and Trying Hard to Remember whether her Birthday was on Tuesday or Wednesday.

Moral.—*Look Impressive.*

MR. BUFFLE, THE YOUNG PERSON, AND
THE SEEDY INDIVIDUAL

MR. BUFFLE, THE YOUNG PERSON, AND
THE SEEDY INDIVIDUAL

∽

MR. BUFFLE was a Barrister of Thirty Years'
Standing, a Bencher of his Inn, and a
Devoted Husband and Father. One Saturday Afternoon Mr. Buffle Sat in his Chambers Working Hard on the Proof-Sheets of the Second Edition
of his Invaluable Work, "The Law Relating to
Vaccination."

At Five O'Clock, Feeling somewhat Exhausted, he
Refreshed himself with a Cup of Tea. It then
Occurred to him that it would be Pleasant to Take a
Stroll in the Beautiful Garden of the Outer Temple
and there Smoke a Cigarette. Mr. Buffle Made for
the Seat under the Catalpa Tree (his Usual Resting-
Place), and Found to his Surprise, that it was Already
Occupied by a Young Person. Mr. Buffle Surmised
that she was a Nursery-Maid, for she was Accompanied by a Perambulator. It also Struck him that
her Appearance was Quite Agreeable. She Wore a
Small Black Bonnet, with Strings Tied in a Bow under
her Chin, a Lilac Print Dress with Spots, and a Very
Becoming Sort of Black Mantle. Mr. Buffle further
Noticed that the Young Person Seemed to be in
Distress; and, as he Drew Near, a Distinct Sob Broke
upon his Ear. Though Elderly, Mr. Buffle was Full
of Gallantry. Seating himself beside the Young Person, he Begged her to Tell him whether he could be

of Any Assistance. The Young Person Replied that she had Just had a Nasty Accident. Which a Splinter from the Pram had Run into her Finger, and the Pain was Somethink Awful, and she didn't Know, she was Sure, how she could Put Up with it Much Longer, and did Mr. Buffle Think he could Find a Doctor? Mr. Buffle Said a Few Comforting Words and Assured the Young Person that he could Deal with the Splinter himself. The Young Person, Still Sobbing, Extended a Plump Hand, and Mr. Buffle without any Difficulty Drew Out the Offending Particle. So Simple was the Operation that Mr. Buffle Rather Wondered why the Young Person had not Performed it herself. After a Little Chat, Mr. Buffle Withdrew to his Chambers and Resumed his Labours. This was Positively All that Happened.

Three Days later a Seedy Individual Waited upon Mr. Buffle in his Chambers. He Explained that he was a Professional Photographer, and was Anxious to Show Mr. Buffle his Collection of Views of the Temple. Mr. Buffle (Feeling a Little Troubled) said he would Greatly Like to See them. The Seedy Individual thereupon Displayed Several Photographs. There was One of Lamb Building, Another of the Middle Temple Hall, a Third of Pump Court, and a Fourth of the Catalpa Tree, with a Close-Up of Mr. Buffle and the Young Person in the Foreground. The Picture had been Taken at a Moment when the Young Person was Looking Exceedingly Coy. Mr. Buffle Looked at the Seedy Individual and the Seedy Individual Looked at Mr. Buffle. After a Pause, Mr. Buffle said he Admired the Photograph of the Catalpa

Tree Enormously, and Asked whether he could Buy not only the Photograph but the Film. The Seedy Individual Agreed that the Photograph of the Catalpa Tree was one of his Most Successful Efforts, but said he was Afraid he could not Part with the Film as he had Contracted to Sell the Copyright to a Newspaper Syndicate. But if Mr. Buffle Thought it was Worth 50*l.* (as he, the Seedy Individual, did) he would Brave the Indignation of the Newspaper Syndicate and Face any Legal Proceedings they might Take. Did Mr. Buffle Hesitate? Not for a Moment. At the Request of the Seedy Individual he Made the Cheque an Open One. Directly the Seedy Individual had Departed, Mr. Buffle Tore the Photograph and the Film into a Thousand Fragments and Flung them Out of the Window. As he did so, he Observed the Seedy Individual and the Young Person in Animated Conversation Hurrying Together in the Direction of the Bank.

Moral.—*Send for the Doctor.*

THE TWO TEMPLARS AND THE LONG
VACATION

THE TWO TEMPLARS AND THE
LONG VACATION

TWO Templars Met at the Railway Station on
their Return from the Long Vacation. The
First Templar had been Shooting and Fishing
in Scotland. The Second Templar had been Doing
the Cathedrals of France and Italy. Each Begged the
Other to Give a Full Account of his Adventures.
The First Templar at once Became Eloquent about
the Wildness of the Birds, the Heavy Cost of Beaters,
and the Discomforts of the Inn to which he had been
Recommended. He also Gave a Spirited Account of
the Salmon he had Lost on the 3rd September, and
the Thirty-Two Pounder he had Landed with a Light
Trout Rod only Last Week. While the First Templar
was Imparting this Information, the Second Templar
was Explaining what a Rough Crossing his Party had
on the 15th August, how Impressed he was with
Chartres, what Gigantic Railway Reforms had been
Carried through by Mussolini, how much he Preferred Assisi to Florence, and how his Wife's Niece
had Unfortunately Contracted Measles in Genoa.
As Neither of them Heard what the Other was Talking about, Both Templars Enjoyed their Chat Immensely. They Ultimately Parted with a Mutual
Threat to Exchange Further and Better Particulars at
a Later Date.

Moral.—*Don't Listen.*

THE CAUTIOUS SOLICITOR AND THE
CHINESE WITNESS

THE CAUTIOUS SOLICITOR AND THE
CHINESE WITNESS

∽

THERE was Once a Solicitor who was both
Learned and Cautious. He never Allowed
Himself to be Taken by Surprise; and he
Invariably had his Tackle in Order. Whilst Pre-
paring for the Trial of a Case of Great Importance,
the Cautious Solicitor Suddenly Realised that Mr.
Chi-Hung-Chang, the Principal Witness for his Client,
was a Chinaman, and that he would have to be Sworn
in Whatever might be the Appropriate Fashion. The
Cautious Solicitor Made Anxious Enquiries and
Gathered that Everything Depended on the Precise
Place of Origin of Mr. Chi-Hung-Chang. It appeared
that if he Came from the Northern Regions the
Breaking of a Saucer was the Central Piece of Ritual;
that if he was from Kwei Chow (or the Parts Adjacent
thereto) he would Require a Lighted Candle which
would be Blown Out at the Critical Moment; and
that if he Happened to be a Native of Kwangsi he
would not Deem himself Properly Sworn Unless and
Until he had Sacrificed a White Cockerel in the Witness Box by Cutting its Throat with a Steel Knife.
The Cautious Solicitor Took no Risks. He Procured
a Dozen Porcelain Saucers of Various Sizes; a Box
of Best Spermaceti Candles and a Box of Superior
Quality Wax Ditto; and (from Leadenhall Market) a
Cockerel of Unblemished Purity, which Spent the

Night in his Bed-Chamber and Inconvenienced him a Great Deal by Crowing Enthusiastically when the Dawn Broke. On the Day Fixed for the Hearing of the Case the Cautious Solicitor Conveyed the Saucers, the Candles, and a Hamper Containing the White Cockerel to the Royal Courts of Justice, and there Awaited the Arrival of the Chinese Witness. When Mr. Chi-Hung-Chang Turned Up he Told the Cautious Solicitor that he had to Catch the Three-Thirty as he was Going to the Grand National. He also Remarked that *Silly Billy's* Price Seemed to have Shortened a Bit. On the Cautious Solicitor Enquiring whether he would Prefer a Saucer, a Lighted Candle, or a Cockerel for the purposes of his Oath, Mr. Chi-Hung-Chang Said he had become a Bit of a Christian Scientist at Balliol, and Thought, on the Whole, he would Like to Affirm. He then Asked the Cautious Solicitor to Come and Have a Drink.

Moral.—*Safety First*.

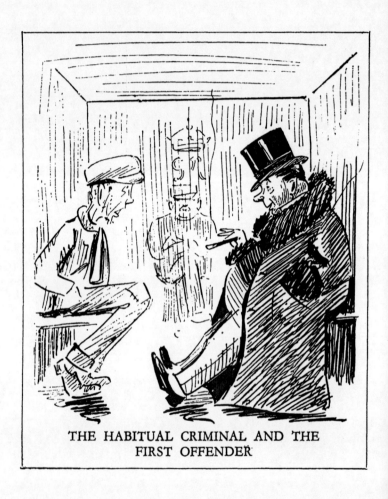

THE HABITUAL CRIMINAL AND THE
FIRST OFFENDER

THE HABITUAL CRIMINAL AND THE
FIRST OFFENDER

∽

ONE Winter's Evening a "Black Maria" Containing a Habitual Criminal and a First Offender was Proceeding from the Old Bailey towards Wormwood Scrubs. The Habitual Criminal Wore a Cloth Cap, and his Lean Neck was Enveloped in a Handkerchief. The First Offender was Richly Dressed and of Portly Build. On his Head he Carried a Silk Hat, and his Overcoat, which was Lined with Mink, had Cuffs and Collar of the Same Admirable Fur. He was Smoking (by Permission of the Kindly Janitor) a Long and Fragrant Corona. Engaging the First Offender in Conversation, the Habitual Criminal Invited his Sympathy. This was his Tenth Conviction for Stealing and Receiving. He was to Do Seven Years' Penal Servitude and Five Years' Preventive Detention. The Habitual Criminal didn't Suppose he had Pinched Fifty Pounds' Worth from First to Last, and he was Jiggered if he hadn't Done Twenty-three Years altogether. Rotten Luck, the Habitual Criminal Called it. The First Offender Gently Demurred. "You Ought," he said, "to have Shown more Restraint. Habitual Criminality is not to be Tolerated. You have only Yourself to Thank for your Present Unhappy Situation." Throwing away his Cigar, the First Offender Proceeded: "Till a Year ago I Led a Blameless Life. Then, having Dissipated my Fortune in Riotous Living, I Started a Bucket-Shop. My Distinguished Appearance and Perfect Manners Enabled me to Rob Widows, Orphans, Clergymen, and University Professors of a Sum Approaching a Hundred Thousand Pounds; and, but for the Treachery of a Trusted Clerk, I should Still be Going Strong. The Judge who Tried me was a Man of Intelligence and Discernment. He very Properly Reminded me that the Disgrace I had Brought upon my Family, my Public School, and my University was in itself a Severe Punishment, and he Directed, as it was my First Offence, that I should be Imprisoned in the Second Division for Six Months." When the Kindly Janitor at last Succeeded in Detaching the Habitual Criminal from the First Offender, the Latter was Suffering from a Contused Eye and a Bleeding Nose. He had also Lost Two Front Teeth.

Moral.—*Be Merciful*.

178

THE ENTHUSIASTIC TOURISTS AND THE
CAPABLE GUIDE

THE ENTHUSIASTIC TOURISTS AND
THE CAPABLE GUIDE

THERE was Once a Party of Tourists who Hailed from Penn., Mass., Ga., Va., and Other Parts of the Land of Freedom and Prohibition. For a Crowded Fortnight they had been Absorbing the Beauties of the Continent and the British Isles. They had Done France, Stratford-on-Avon, Switzerland, the English Lakes and Cathedrals, Italy, the Flemish Battlefields, the Old Curiosity Shop, the Rhine, the Cheshire Cheese, and the Houses of Parliament. Now, Exhausted but Still Enthusiastic, they were Visiting the Temple. Happily they had Discovered a Capable Guide who could Show Them Everything that was worthy of Notice. First, the Capable Guide Took Them to the Law Courts where King Charles the First and "Bardell *v.* Pickwick" were Tried. Next he Pointed out Pump Court, where Charles Lamb Wrote the "Vicar of Wakefield." In the Garden of the Middle Temple They Saw the Exact Spot (now Occupied by a Concrete Vase Containing Geraniums) where Peace was Signed by King Richard the Third after the Battle of Evesham. And, Finally, he Led them to the Terrace Flanking the Inner Temple Hall, that they might Inspect the Very Rings to which Queen Elizabeth's Barge was Tied Up when Her Majesty Came to Dine with the Benchers of the Honourable Society. The Tourists with Tears of Gratitude in Their Eyes Heaped Largesse upon the Capable Guide.

Moral.—*Miss Nothing.*

THE CAREFUL JUNIOR AND THE
LEADING QUESTION

THE CAREFUL JUNIOR AND THE
LEADING QUESTION
~

ACAREFUL Junior Read his First Brief Again
and Again till he Knew its Contents by Heart.
He also Took the Precaution of Making
Marginal Notes on the Various Proofs of the Wit-
nesses. Thus, he Reasoned, he Could Bring Out the
Evidence with Clarity and Effect if it Should Fall to
his Lot to Examine Anybody in Chief. In Due
Course the Leader Requested him to Take Alfred
Grubby, the Independent Witness who had Viewed
the Accident through the Window of the "Golden
Unicorn." The Careful Junior Rose Trembling to
his Feet. The Judge having Written Down the
Name of the Witness, the Careful Junior, Reading
from his Proof, Asked Alfred Grubby whether he
Lived at 48, West Beaconsfield Rise, Tiptree Avenue,
Clerkenwell. To the Careful Junior's Horror and
Dismay the Witness Furiously Answered in the Nega-
tive. With a Cry of Distress the Careful Junior Sunk
Unconscious to the Ground.

*   *   *   *   *

Three Days Later the Careful Junior was Aware of
the Roar of Traffic, a Strong Smell of Cabbage, and
the Angry Voices of Ministering Angels. He was in
a Nursing Home. When the Careful Junior was
Well Enough to Discuss Things he was Informed that
Alfred Grubby's Furious Demeanour was Due to the
Fact that he had Changed his Address after his Proof
had been Taken.

Moral.—*Never Lead the Witness.*

THE ATHLETIC TEMPLARS WHO CLIMBED
THE DENT DU CHIEN

THE ATHLETIC TEMPLARS WHO
CLIMBED THE DENT DU CHIEN

༄

TWO Athletic Templars, the Long Vacation
having Set In, Proceeded to the Alps as Soon as
Their Respective Clerks Permitted them to Do
So. For they were Keen Mountaineers. The Ath-
letic Templars Rejoiced in their Freedom. They
Laughed Aloud to Think that they had Left Behind
them Solicitors, Briefs, Managing Clerks, Statements
of Claim, and all the Paraphernalia of the Law.
Arrived in Switzerland they Determined to Do, Once
More, the Dear Old *Dent du Chien* by the Difficult
Route. Across the Glacier, Leaving the *Cuisine du
Cardinal* on the Left, Skirting the Moraine, and so Up
the South-West Face. Did the Athletic Templars
Enjoy the Climb? Of Course they Did. Did they
Discuss the Beauty of the Eternal Peaks and the Glory
of the Untrodden Snows? By No Means. For the
First Four Hours they Debated whether the Judgment
of the Court of Appeal in *Finkelheim* v. *Cohenstein* was
Correct. Between the Hut and the Summit (Eight
Hours) they Compared the Forensic Giants of the
Past with the Pigmies of To-day. And During the

Descent (Six Hours) they Speculated as to the Judicial Changes which would Probably Take Place in the Month of October.

Moral.—*Have a Change.*

THE PRUDENT JUDGE AND THE STOUT USHER

THE PRUDENT JUDGE AND THE
STOUT USHER

∽

A GREAT Many Years Ago there Lived a Prudent Judge who Gave Universal Satisfaction. He was a Magnificent Lawyer. Legal Problems, however Complicated and Obscure, Never Caused him the Least Alarm. When the Doctrine of Equitable Subrogation was Mentioned, the Prudent Judge Brightened Up; and Such Topics as Anticipatory Breach of the Contract, the Provisions of the Harter Act, and Covenants Running with the Land Filled him with Joy. And, Wonderful to Relate, the Prudent Judge was Just as Good when it Came to a Question of Fact. As the Prudent Judge was a Bachelor and a Recluse, whose Practice at the Bar had been of the Stuffiest Description, there Appeared to be no Reason for this Phenomenon. But there was. Quite Early in his Judicial Career the Prudent Judge Detected that the Stout Usher in his Court was a Person of Great Good Sense. He therefore Summoned the Stout Usher to his Room, Pressed a Substantial Offering into his Hand, and Begged him to Abandon his Habit of Sleeping throughout the Proceedings, and to Pay Close Attention to the Evidence in Each Case. The Stout Usher Orally Agreed so to Do. Thereafter, when the Court Adjourned, the Prudent Judge would Ask the Stout Usher what he Thought about the Various Witnesses.

The Stout Usher was Never in Doubt. Sometimes he would Say that the Plaintiff was a Bit of a Liar; on Other Occasions he would Pick Out the Defendant as the Ananias of the Piece. Under the Able Guidance of the Stout Usher the Prudent Judge Never Went Wrong. And when At Last the Prudent Judge Retired, the Attorney-General, in a Valedictory Address, Dwelt upon his Uncanny Knowledge of Human Nature and his Marvellous Capacity for Distinguishing Truth from Fiction.

Moral.—*Ask the Usher.*

THE THREE ELDERLY JURISTS WHO MET
AFTER MANY YEARS

THE THREE ELDERLY JURISTS WHO
MET AFTER MANY YEARS

ᔍ

THREE Elderly Jurists who had been Friends in their Youth Met after Many Years. The Career of Each had been Distinguished. The First, whose Treatise on the "Laws and Customs of the Khojas of the Himalaya Foot-Hills" (Based upon the *Rajatarangini,* as Summarised by Abu'l Fazl in the *A'in-i-Akbari*) is Quoted wherever the Kashmiri Tongue is Spoken, had Held High Office in the East. The Second, after Filling a Law-Officership with Glittering Efficiency, had Climbed to the Topmost Rung of the Legal Ladder at Home. The Third by his Activities as a Parliamentary Draftsman had Earned the Execrations of Several Generations of Practising Lawyers. The Three Elderly Jurists Agreed to Dine together and Collate their Varied Experiences. They Duly Forgathered and Feasted. Did they Discuss the Bureaucratic Tendencies of Modern Legislation, the Hindu Law of Succession in Zanzibar, or the Question of the Lord Chancellor's Retiring Pension? Yes; for About Ten Minutes. Then they Turned to Other Topics. With the Whitebait they were Recalling Happy Evenings they had Severally Spent in the Defunct Music-Halls of the Metropolis. While Consuming the Joint they Compared the Respective Charms of Miss Violet Cameron, Miss Sylvia Grey and Miss Florence St. John. At the Liqueur Stage of the Proceedings they were Endeavouring (with Some Success) to Reproduce the Words and the Melody of "Two Lovely Black Eyes." And when the Waiter came to Remind them that the Club Closed at One-Thirty, the Three Elderly Jurists were Cordially Agreeing that the Elegant Figure of Miss Nellie Farren in "Little Jack Sheppard" was the Most Precious of all their Memories.

Moral.—*Think Deeply.*

THE NERVOUS YOUTH WHO DID HIS BEST IN
THE CIRCUMSTANCES

THE NERVOUS YOUTH WHO DID
HIS BEST IN THE CIRCUMSTANCES

∽

A NERVOUS Youth, after Waiting and Watching for Many Months, Received his First County Court Brief. The Brief Conveyed to the Nervous Youth that he was to Appear for the Plaintiff, a Merchant in Whitechapel, who Considered that he was Entitled to Commission on the Sale of a Fish-and-Chips Establishment in the Mile End Road. It Seemed, also, that there was Some Doubt as to whether the Claim was Well-Founded, and that the Utmost Discretion in Handling the Plaintiff's Case would be Necessary if a Satisfactory Result was to be Secured. The Nervous Youth Repaired to the County Court, Determined to Do or Die. Owing to the Slow Progress of the Bus in which he Performed his Journey, the Nervous Youth Found, on his Arrival, that he had Kept the Court Waiting and that the Judge was Considerably Ruffled. Much Agitated by the Sharpness of the Judge's Comments, the Nervous Youth Rose to his Feet, to Find that he was Afflicted by a Sudden Condition of Aphasia and Loss of Memory. The Nervous Youth has no Distinct Recollection of what Happened Next; but from the Account of the Proceedings Given to Him by Bystanders, the Nervous Youth Understands that in Faltering Tones he Read Aloud to the Jury the First Two Pages of his Brief, and that, when he Came to the Bit which Recommended that he had Better not Call the Plaintiff, as he had Been in Prison More than Once, the Jury had Stopped the Case.

Moral.—*Take a Taxi.*

THE AGED JUDGE WHO REMEMBERED THE
PAST AND CHANGED HIS MIND

THE AGED JUDGE
WHO REMEMBERED THE PAST AND
CHANGED HIS MIND

∽

ONE Hot Afternoon an Aged Judge Found Himself Growing More and More Irritable as a Tedious Case Dragged On. The Youthful Counsel who Represented the Plaintiff was Nervous and Incoherent. Also he Entirely Declined to Shorten the Proceedings by Adopting the Various Hints offered by the Aged Judge. Stung to Madness, the Aged Judge was About to Let Himself Go and Tell the Youthful Counsel Exactly what he Thought about him, when he Suddenly Remembered an Incident of the Past. The Aged Judge Recalled the Occasion, Fifty Years Ago, when he Held his First Brief; the Savage Appearance of the Judge; his own Terror; his Rage and Humiliation when the Judge Informed him that he didn't Know his Business; the Sleepless Night which Followed; and the Misery of the Lady of his Choice when he Told her all about It. Therefore the Aged Judge Restrained himself; and when, at Long Last, the Case Came to an End, he Declared (Quite Untruly) that he had been Greatly Assisted by the Arguments of the Youthful Counsel, and that the Plaintiff had been Fortunate to Secure his Services. What was the Result? The Youthful Counsel Left the Court in Wild Elation; the Father of his True Love was So Impressed by the Report of the Case in the Papers that he Withdrew his Opposition to the Engagement; and the Youthful Counsel and his Future Bride Invested the Fee (Five and One) in a Lunch at the Savoy, an Arm-Chair, and a Coal-Scuttle. And when the Aged Judge Heard how Fruitful his Kindness had been, he Burst into Tears and Sent the Young People a Handsome Gift.

Moral.—*Remember the Past*.

THE LITIGANTS IN PERSON WHO COMPARED
NOTES

THE LITIGANTS IN PERSON WHO
COMPARED NOTES

∾

TWO Litigants in Person met in the Vaults of the Royal Courts of Justice. Each was Anxious for Refreshment after his Oratorical Efforts. The Lunatic Ordered Roast Potatoes, Two Cold Muffins, and a Double Whisky. The Scientist Thought he would have a Chop. The Litigants in Person then Compared Notes. The Lunatic was Very Happy. It Appeared that, Finding his Incarceration Irksome, he had Escaped from the Asylum in the Laundry Basket. It had then Occurred to him that he was Sane. He therefore Brought Actions against the Doctors who had Certified him (for Negligence) and all his Near Relations (for Conspiracy). No Solicitor would Take up his Case, so he had Appeared in Person. The Judge had been Charming and the Jury Most Sympathetic. In fact, they had Just Awarded him 10,000*l*. Damages. The Scientist Congratulated the Lunatic and Took up the Running. Some Years ago he had Invented a New Explosive. The Dishonest Representative of a Government Department had Stolen it, Used it, and Denied having Done so. The Scientist, Advised by Eminent Lawyers, had Proceeded by Way of Petition of Right and had been Told by the Court that he Ought to have Sued in Tort. Now (as his Money was Gone) he had Sued in Tort in Person and had been Defeated. The

Judge had Suggested to the Jury that he had a Bee in his Bonnet, and the Jury had Stopped the Case. The Lunatic Expressed his Sorrow, and after Firmly Declining to Pay his Bill and Embracing the Waitress, Fled from the Dining-Room. The Scientist Proceeded to his Lodgings in a Bus. The Same Evening the Lunatic Blew his Brains Out because the Asylum Authorities Refused to Re-Admit him, and the Scientist was Taken to the Workhouse.

Moral.—*Lex Lunaticos Amat.*

MR. TITMOUSE, MRS. TITMOUSE, AND THE
CLAIM FOR GOODS SOLD AND DELIVERED

MR. TITMOUSE, MRS. TITMOUSE, AND THE CLAIM FOR GOODS SOLD AND DELIVERED

∽

MR. TITMOUSE, of Pump-Handle Court, was a Barrister and a Happily Married Man. There was but One Fly in the Ointment. Mrs. Titmouse, though Amiable and of Pleasing Appearance, was not a Capable Manager, and Mr. Titmouse Often had Occasion to Complain of her Reckless Expenditure. At last, Mr. Titmouse was Driven to Take the Extreme Course of Putting his Foot Down. Mrs. Titmouse Gathered that if she were County-Courted, she would Jolly Well have to Get the Money out of her Own People. Nor did the Tears of Mrs. Titmouse Cause him to Recede from this Position. A Few Days Later Mr. Titmouse, Armed with a Three and One, was in the Robing-Room of the County-Court which Enjoys Jurisdiction over West Kensington and the Parts Adjacent thereto. To his Delight a Solicitor's Clerk Pressed another Brief into his Hand, Saying that the Case had been Called On and that his Counsel had been Held Up Elsewhere. The Claim, he Explained, was by Messrs. Lingerie, Ltd., for the Price of Goods Sold and Delivered and there was No Defence. Mr. Titmouse Rushed into Court to Find that the Defendant was already in the Witness-Box. She was Conversing Very Sweetly with the Judge. It was Mrs. Titmouse.

Before Mr. Titmouse could Open his Mouth the Judge said he had Ascertained from the Defendant that the Goods in Question had been Ordered on behalf of her Husband, and he Supposed there was no Objection to Substituting him as the Defendant. Mr. Titmouse was so Taken Aback that he Feebly Assented to this Proposal. Judgment was Accordingly Signed against Mr. Titmouse (whose Christian Names Mrs. Titmouse Obligingly Supplied) with Costs. When he Got Home that Evening Mr. Titmouse Took the Line that he had been Moved to this Act of Self-Sacrifice by Pity for Mrs. Titmouse, and Mrs. Titmouse was So Tactful that she Pretended to Believe Him.

Moral.—*Be Firm.*

THE DEAF REPORTER, THE DILIGENT YOUNG
COUNSEL, AND THE GLORIOUS WIN

THE DEAF REPORTER, THE DILIGENT YOUNG COUNSEL, AND THE GLORIOUS WIN

∽

THERE was Once an Old Gentleman who Practised as a Special Pleader in the Early Part of the Eighteenth Century. Being Very Deaf and Extremely Stupid, he Thought he would Take to Reporting. His Reports, by Reason of his Above-Mentioned Disabilities, were Shockingly Bad. As his Contemporaries Knew that the Old Gentleman Heard One Half of the Case and Reported the Other, they Paid No Attention to his Efforts. When the Deaf Reporter had Produced One Volume he Passed Away, much Regretted by his Laundress, to whom (according to Some) he was Secretly Married. Two Hundred Years Rolled by, and a Diligent Young Counsel, who was Accustomed to Go to the Root of Things, Unearthed the Forgotten Volume. To his Joy he Discovered therein an Authority which Exactly Fitted the Difficult Case he had to Argue on the Morrow in the County Court. The Startling Proposition Contained in the Head-Note was Due to the Fact that the Deaf Reporter had Omitted the Word "Not" when Taking Down the Observations of Mr. Justice Punt in the Court of Common Pleas. The Diligent Young Counsel Waited till the County Court Judge Showed Signs of Wobbling and then Loosed Off his Splendid Find. The County Court

Judge, who was Anxious to Catch his Train, was in no Critical Mood. Thus the Diligent Young Counsel had a Glorious Win and Sowed the Seeds of a Large and Lucrative Practice.

Moral.—*Si Auctoritatem Requiris Circumspice.*

THE DISTINGUISHED ARCHITECT AND THE
PALACE OF JUSTICE

THE DISTINGUISHED ARCHITECT
AND THE PALACE OF JUSTICE

THERE was Once a Distinguished Architect who Won an Open Competition for the Best Design for a Palace of Justice. He was an R.A. His Plans Carried Out the Best Architectural Traditions. The Palace of Justice, which Cost Several Millions, was in the Norman-Jacobean-Early-English Style. Each of the Thirty Courts was Extremely Lofty. The Gallery for the Waiting Jurors was Approached by a Tortuous Stairway. The Jury-Box was a Structure into which the Twelve Good Men and True could Just Fit if they Held their Breath. The Judge's Seat was Half-Way up the Wall. The Seats for Counsel were so Arranged that they Could not Get In or Out without Injuring Each Other; and the Desks so Sloped that their Briefs and Papers Fell to the Floor unless Held on by Main Force. The Witness Occupied a Box so Far Removed from both Counsel and the Jury that the Witness had to Shout his Answers if he was to be Heard. The Doors Clapped Noisily when they were Opened or Shut. The Floors Contained Concealed Steps down which the Unwary Fell with a Crash. Everybody Agreed that the Palace of Justice was a Miserable Failure. When a Great Many Years had Gone by the Palace of Justice, owing to some Defect in its Patent Heating Apparatus, was Burned to the

Ground. There was Universal Rejoicing, for it was Felt that now At Last the Errors of the Distinguished Architect Could be Put Right. Were they? They were Not. The Authorities Unearthed the Distinguished Architect (now in a State of Senile Decay) and Paid him an Immense Sum of Money to Reproduce his Old Plans. Thus the New Palace of Justice Proved to be the Twin of its Predecessor, except that the Courts were Ten Feet Higher and the Judge was Placed Still Nearer to the Ceiling.

Moral.—*It Might be Worse.*

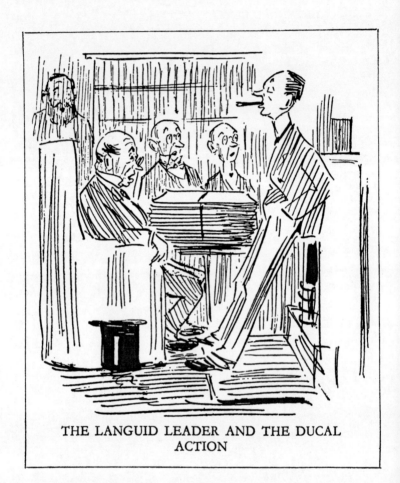

THE LANGUID LEADER AND THE DUCAL
ACTION

THE LANGUID LEADER AND THE
DUCAL ACTION

〜

THERE was Once a Languid Leader. He
Despised Old-Fashioned Methods and did not
Think Much of his Contemporaries. Though
the Languid Leader was both Learned and Industrious
he Preferred to Pose as a Dilettante. Sometimes he
Remarked that he Only Practised at the Bar because it
Provided him with a Certain Amount of Pocket-
Money. Often he would Say that it was an Old
Woman's Job. Shortly after the Languid Leader had
Taken Silk a Painful Dispute Arose between the
Bogglesdale Rural District Council and Duke of
Agincourt. The Rural District Council Asserted,
and the Duke Denied, that there was a Right of Way
over his Grace's Best Grouse-Moor. As the Passage
of Citizens along the Sky-Line would Absolutely
Ruin the Third and Fourth Drives the Duke Con-
sulted his Family Solicitor and a Chancery Action was
Duly Launched. The Duke Retained Mr. Topnot,
K.C., the Great Real Property Lawyer, to Present his
Claim for Damages, a Declaration and an Injunc-
tion. The Rural District Council Delivered a
Defence and Counterclaim which Bristled with Law
and Fact. Two Days before the Case Came On, Mr.
Topnot, K.C., was Attacked by Influenza and
Returned his Large and Well-Marked Brief. Con-
sternation Reigned in the Ducal Camp. The Family

Solicitor, not without Misgivings, Approached the Clerk of the Languid Leader. That Experienced Official Undertook that if the Fee was Substantially Increased (as Time was so Short) his Employer would Give the Matter his Close Attention. On the Eve of the Day Appointed for the Trial the Duke of Agincourt, the Family Solicitor, the Managing Clerk, and the Junior Counsel Attended at the Chambers of the Languid Leader for the Final Consultation. The Languid Leader had Studied the Brief with Care and Knew the Case Inside Out. But he was not Going to Give the Show Away. He Received the Party with Vague Cordiality and Thought it Well to Mistake the Duke of Agincourt for the Managing Clerk. He then Observed that he had Only been Able to Glance at the Pleadings, and Opined that the Case was about a Cargo of Chinese Pickled Eggs. When this Misapprehension was Rectified the Languid Leader Exhibited no Emotion. After the Junior Counsel had Explained the Outstanding Points, the Languid Leader Yawned and Said he was Afraid he must be Going to the House. The Duke of Agincourt Left the Consultation Speechless with Rage and Indignation. On the Morrow the Languid Leader Delivered a Dashing Speech and Cross-Examined the Defendants' Witnesses into Cocked Hats. When All was Happily Over the Languid Leader Received the Congratulations of the Duke of Agincourt with Easy Nonchalance. He Explained that One Case was Much Like Another and that it was Quite Easy to Pick a Thing Up as You Went Along.

Moral.—*Keep It Up.*

THE WISE OLD BIRD WHO RETIRED

THE WISE OLD BIRD WHO RETIRED

THERE was Once a Wise Old Bird who Retired from the Bench the Very Moment he had Done his Fifteen Years. The Wise Old Bird's Friends Assured him he would be Bored to Tears. They also Hinted Darkly that, Deprived of his Customary Employment, he would Probably Pass Away in the Near Future. Were they Right in their Gloomy Prognostications? Did he Miss the Dear Old Courts of Justice? Not a Bit of it. The Wise Old Bird took a Nice Little Place in the Country, and Thought Out an Admirable Routine. He Rose Late, Breakfasted Comfortably, Read *The Times* (Skipping the Law Reports) and had a Look at the Pigs. Then he Lunched and Read a Novel. At Four-Thirty the Wise Old Bird Took a Cup of Tea and had Another Look at the Pigs. At Seven-Thirty he Dined, Finishing Up with Two Glasses of Vintage Port, an Old Brandy, and a Cigar. Before Retiring to Rest he Consumed a Stiff Whisky and Soda, and had Another if he Felt he Wanted it. When in Need of Society he Invited his Niece Emily for the Week-End, but he Always Expected her to Go Home by the Ten-Forty on Monday. The Wise Old Bird Firmly Declined to be Bothered with Quarter Sessions, Petty Sessions, or Any Nonsense of that Kind. He thus Survived to Celebrate his Ninety-Eighth Birthday and had the Extreme Satisfaction of Outliving All his Contemporaries.

Moral.—*Retire*.

THE GREAT LAWYER WHO TOLD HIS
AUDIENCE HOW TO DO IT

THE GREAT LAWYER WHO TOLD HIS AUDIENCE HOW TO DO IT

∽

A GREAT Lawyer Once Attended a Banquet. He was the Principal Guest. The Great Lawyer's Hosts were Budding Members of the Bar who had Formed a Debating Society. They Desired to Pay Honour where Honour was Due and to Learn from One who had Arrived at the Top how the Trick was to be Done. The Great Lawyer, when Responding to the Toast of the Evening, Told them All About It. Individual Effort and Concentration, said the Great Lawyer, were the Only Things that Counted. There were Some, he Believed, who Thought that Luck was an Important Factor in Life. They were Wrong. He who Wished to Succeed must Work—Work—Work. He must Rise Early and Map Out his Day. He must be an Athlete in Strict Training. He must be a Sentry at his Post, Morning, Noon and Night. He must Serve One Master, and One Master Only—his Profession. The Great Lawyer Reminded them of the Emperor Napoleon's Observations on the Subject of Knapsacks and Bâtons, and Assured them that, if Only they would Fight the Good Fight, Each One of them might be a Marshal in the Army of the Law. And in a Moving Peroration the Great Lawyer Attributed his Own Success in Life to a Strict Adherence to the Maxims he was Expounding. In Point of Fact, the Great

Lawyer had been Spoon-Fed by a Near Relative from the Day of his Call; he had Always Taken Things Easily and Done himself Well; he had made a Matrimonial Alliance which Furnished him with Abundant Cash; a Series of Unexpected Political Events had Floated him into a Government; and the Sudden Demise of an Important Personage on the Eve of his Party's Defeat at the Polls had Provided him with the Fat Job which he now Enjoyed. When the Great Lawyer Resumed his seat after Speaking for Forty-Five Minutes, his Innocent Hosts Cheered him to the Echo, and Went Home Grimly Determined to Follow in the Great Lawyer's Footsteps.

Moral.—*Say the Right Thing.*

THE EXPERIENCED JUDGE, THE RUNNING
DOWN CASE, AND THE LAW RELATING TO
CONTRIBUTORY NEGLIGENCE

THE EXPERIENCED JUDGE, THE
RUNNING DOWN CASE, AND THE
LAW RELATING TO CONTRIBUTORY
NEGLIGENCE

∽

THERE was Once an Experienced Judge who Tried a Running-Down Case. The Defendant Pleaded that the Said Accident was Due to the Negligence or Alternatively the Contributory Negligence of the Plaintiff. The Experienced Judge (who was a Person of Robust Intellect) Requested the Jury to Say whether the Disaster in Question was Caused by the Negligence of the Plaintiff or by that of the Defendant. As the Result of an Application for a New Trial the Experienced Judge Gathered that he had Failed to Explain Sufficiently to the Jury the Law Relating to Contributory Negligence. Shortly Afterwards the Experienced Judge had Another Running-Down Case to Try. This Time he Determined there should be no Mistake about the Law. So he Told the Retired Draper, the Lady in Glasses, the Dejected Publican, and the Nine Others who Composed the Jury All About It. They were, he said, to Consider whether (if they Thought that the Motor had in fact been Guilty of Contributory Negligence) the Taxi-Cab could by the Exercise of Reasonable Care have Avoided the Consequences of Such Contributory Negligence. Further, they Must Ask themselves whether it was the Motor or the Taxi-Cab which had the Last Opportunity of Avoiding the Negligence of the Other. Thirdly, they must Enquire whether the Negligence of the Motor, or that of the Taxi-Cab, could be Deemed to be the Proximate, as Distinguished from the Remote, Cause of the Plaintiff's Injuries. Fourthly, they must Tell him whether they Regarded the Negligence of Either as the Efficient or Decisive Cause of The Accident. Lastly, they Must Bear in Mind that if the Confusion of the Driver of the Motor had been Induced by the Want of Skill and Caution on the Part of the Taxi-Cab they should Give Due Weight to that Fact in Forming an Opinion as to the Degree of Responsibility which must be Attributed to the Former. The Experienced Judge then Read to the Jury at Length Various Relevant Cases Contained in the Law Reports including *Dublin, Wicklow & Wexford Railway Co.* v. *Slattery*, 3 App. Cas. 1155; *Radley* v. *L. & N.W. Railway Co.*, 1 App. Cas. 759; and *The Bernina*, 12 P. D. 36. He Finished Up with the Speeches of Their Lordships in *The Volute* [1922] 1 A. C. 129, Adding, however, the Warning that the Jury might Disregard the Provisions of the Maritime Conventions Act, 1911. After an Absence of Four Hours the Jury Announced that there was no Hope of their Agreement. As the Plaintiff's Financial Resources were Now Exhausted the Case gave no Further Trouble.

Moral.—*Explain the Law to the Jury.*

THE MAN OF AFFAIRS, THE INTELLIGENT
SOLICITOR, AND THE PROMISING SON

THE MAN OF AFFAIRS, THE INTELLIGENT SOLICITOR, AND THE PROMISING SON

∽

A MAN of Affairs had a Promising Son to Whom he was Devotedly Attached and whose Material Advancement in this Vale of Tears he Fondly Desired. Therefore when the Man of Affairs Next had Occasion to Consult his Solicitor (a Person of Lively Intelligence) he Suggested—Quite Tactfully—at the Close of the Interview that the Solicitor should Send his Son a Brief at the Earliest Possible Moment. The Man of Affairs Added that his Son was a Youth of Parts in whom the Intelligent Solicitor might Repose Absolute Confidence. The Intelligent Solicitor with Cheerful Alacrity said he would At Once Brief the Youth in Question in a Case of Vital Importance, then Pending, in which the Man of Affairs was the Defendant. With a Cry of Agony the Man of Affairs Told him to Do Nothing of the Kind.

Moral.—*Charity Begins at Home.*

MABEL GUDGEON, THE DRESSMAKER'S BILL,
UNCLE PETER AND THE ARTICLED CLERK

MABEL GUDGEON, THE DRESSMAKER'S BILL, UNCLE PETER AND THE ARTICLED CLERK

∽

MABEL GUDGEON, a Beautiful Orphan, Resided with her Uncle Peter in Regent's Park. Uncle Peter was the Senior Partner in the Firm of Gudgeon, Gudgeon & Co. No Solicitor was More Respected in the City of London; but it has to be Admitted that Mabel Sometimes Found him Rather a Grumpy Companion. One Morning, at Breakfast, Mabel was Shocked to Receive a Peremptory Demand for Payment from her Dressmaker. The Figure at the Bottom of the Account Made her Sit Up. She was Still more Horrified when Uncle Peter Required her to Produce the Document for his Inspection. As soon as Uncle Peter had Recovered his Calm he Telephoned for Young Mr. Pott, the New Articled Clerk, and Told him to Settle with Madame Fleurette At Once. Meanwhile Mabel Wept. Young Mr. Pott Came Back in No Time to Say that Madame Fleurette (who was in Fact a Stout Hebrew of the Male Sex) had Agreed to Knock Off Thirty-Three Per Cent. in Consideration of an Immediate Cash Payment. Mabel Rewarded Young Mr. Pott (who was of Good Appearance) with a Tearful but Very Sweet Smile. So Pleased was Uncle Peter that he Asked Young Mr. Pott to Dinner. Can you Guess the Sequel? At First Uncle Peter would not Hear of It; but when he Learned that Young Mr. Pott's Father was a Wealthy Manufacturer of Glue, who had Recently been Made a Baronet, his Opposition Weakened.   Uncle Peter then Insisted on a Long Engagement; but After Enduring the Engagement for Six Weeks he Insisted on a Short One.   So Henry (for Such was his Christian Name) and Mabel were Married at St. Jude's.   It was a Very Pretty Wedding, and the Four Bridesmaids Wore Tight-Fitting Bodices, Tulle Skirts and Court Shoes (All Pink). Mr. and Mrs. Pott at First Occupied a Flat near Earl's Court Station.   But Soon, Prompted by Happy Expectations, they Secured a Roomier Abode with Good Nursery Accommodation.   And now, Any Morning, Mrs. Pott may be Seen with her String-Bag Shopping Like Anything at John Barker's.

Moral.—*You Never Can Tell.*

MR. SHARP, MR. BRIGHT, AND THE AWARD
STATED IN THE FORM OF A SPECIAL CASE

MR. SHARP, MR. BRIGHT, AND THE
AWARD STATED IN THE FORM
OF A SPECIAL CASE

∽

MR. SHARP and Mr. Bright, though Barristers-at-law of Twelve Months' Standing, had Positively Nothing to Do. They Decided that it was Essential to Get a Move on. As Clients were so Shy some Public Demonstration of their Learning and Ability Clearly had to be Made. Having Put their Heads together, Mr. Sharp and Mr. Bright Hit Upon an Admirable Plan. Their Clerk should State an Award in the Form of a Special Case. The Facts should be of Intense Human Interest and the Problems Arising therefrom should be Complicated and Obscure. They would Prepare the Arguments on Either Side with the Utmost Care; the Special Case should be Set Down for Hearing; and, Instructed by Friendly Young Solicitors (whom they could Readily Discover), Mr. Sharp and Mr. Bright would Electrify the Court. There was no Reason why the Case should not be Carried to the House of Lords. All Went Well. The Special Case, Skilfully Drafted by Mr. Sharp and Mr. Bright, was Set Down (at a Trifling Cost) for Hearing in the Special Paper. It was a Masterpiece. The Incidents Narrated were Thrilling but Improbable. The Robust Style of Mr. Edgar Wallace was Wedded to the Quaint Fancy of Robert Louis Stevenson. A Marriage, Invalid by the Law of England, but Valid by the Law of Tibet (in which Country the Wife had been Domiciled as an Infant), had Resulted in the Birth of an Expectant Heir. After Mortgaging his Reversion to his Mother's Tibetan Estates to a Money-Lender the Expectant Heir had Insured his Life. The Policy he had Assigned to a Person who (Intending his Death) Chartered an Unseaworthy Yacht in which the Expectant Heir was Drowned. Before being Drowned the Expectant Heir (when Slightly Intoxicated) had Made a Will Devising the Mortgaged Lands to a Society for the Abolition of Gaming, Wagering and Church Establishments. The Mother of the Expectant Heir had then Married a Clergyman in Shropshire who Obtained a Divorce ai 1 thereafter Married the Money-Lender's Widow. 1 e Opinion of the Court was Asked upon the Various Nice Questions to which these and other Collateral Events Gave Rise. Unfortunately When Mr. Sharp Rose to Argue on behalf of the Claimants, the Judge Said that Large Sums Appeared to be Owing to the Revenue for Stamps; that the Case ought to Go Back to the Arbitrator for his Finding upon Several Matters which he had Left Obscure; and that he would Send all the Papers to the Director of Public Prosecutions in order that the Criminal Law might be Set in Motion. Thus the Labours of Mr. Sharp and Mr. Bright were Wasted.

Moral.—*Stick to the County Court.*

THE DISGRUNTLED PRACTITIONER WHO
THOUGHT POORLY OF EVERYBODY

THE DISGRUNTLED PRACTITIONER
WHO THOUGHT POORLY OF
EVERYBODY

∽

THERE was Once a Disgruntled Practitioner who Complained Loudly of Everybody. Whilst he was a Junior he Thought very Poorly of the Leaders. The Disgruntled Practitioner Wondered why such a Collection of Gumps were ever Briefed at all. After a Case had been Disposed of he would Remark that the Blighter had Made a Mess of it, or that the Ass had Thrown Away the Verdict, or that the Idiot had not Understood the Point. After the Disgruntled Practitioner had Taken Silk he Discovered that the Juniors were, without Exception, Half-Wits who Expected him to Do their Work for them. In the Fullness of Time the Disgruntled Practitioner became a Judge. Now he Found that his Colleagues were Mostly Duds and that the Court of Appeal (which Often Reversed him) was Deplorably Weak. He Often Explained to his Clerk that the Legal System of the Country was Doomed, for, Bad as the Bench was, there was Nobody at the Bar who was Fit for Promotion to a Judgeship. His Clerk, who had his own Views on the Subject, Respectfully Agreed with him. But when the Disgruntled Practitioner at last Disappeared it didn't Seem to Matter very Much, and the Legal System Got on Quite Comfortably without him.

Moral.—*Cheer Up.*

THE BARONY OF DE MONTAZURE AND
FRONT-DE-BŒUF, THE COMMITTEE FOR
PRIVILEGES, AND THE SWEET YOUNG LADY

THE BARONY OF DE MONTAZURE AND FRONT-DE-BŒUF, THE COMMITTEE FOR PRIVILEGES, AND THE SWEET YOUNG LADY

∽

THE Barony of De Montazure and Front-De-Bœuf had long been in Abeyance. Whether the Original Baron De Montazure and Front-de-Bœuf had Ever been Summoned to the Parliament of King Edward III, Holden at Wallingford in the Year 1369, was a Matter of Debate. Indeed, Some Peerage Lawyers of Note Declared that the Nobleman in Question had Never Existed, while Others Held that the Alleged Parliament was in Fact a Court Heriot Summoned by the Local Lord of the Manor to Determine the Ownership of a Cow which had Estrayed upon the Waste thereof, and that its One and Only Statute (*De Vacca Detinenda*, 43 Ed. 3, c. 6, Ruff. Stat.) Merely Embodied the Order of that Tribunal "Qe Vache Soit Detenuz en Prisone."[1] Therefore there was Much Interest Amongst Antiquarians when Miss Smythe-Bilkington-Smythe Put Forward her Claim to have the Abeyance Terminated in her Favour as The Baron De Montazure and Front-de-Bœuf's Senior Co-Heiress. She had Wisely Placed her Affairs in the Hands of a Highly Competent Solicitor. The Highly Competent Solicitor Kept a Good Publicity Department, and was Careful to Let the Newspapers Know that Miss Smythe-Bilkington-

[1] See Cott. M.S. 64, § 11, and Rot. Wall. temp. Ed. Tert.

Smythe was not only a Keen Hockey Player, but a Splendid Swimmer and Devoted to Dogs; also, that she would Attend the Hearing of her Claim. When the Parties Appeared at the Bar of the House of Lords the Members of the Committee for Privileges were Present in Full Force. They were Delighted with the Appearance of the Sweet Young Lady who Sat in the Pen Reserved for Counsel. Her Bobbed Hair, her Slender Figure, her Large Grey Eyes, and her Winsome Dignity were Indeed Calculated to Touch the Stoniest Heart. The Sweet Young Lady Paid the Closest Attention to the Proceedings, and from Time to Time Assisted Counsel by Producing the Necessary Year Book, Parliament Roll, or What-Not. On the Afternoon of the Second Day their Lordships were Concerned to Note that the Sweet Young Lady Shewed Signs of Faintness, and the Senior Lord of Appeal Directed the Attendant to Provide her with a Glass of Water. At the Close of the Arguments the Committee, by a Majority of One, Declared that Miss Smythe-Bilkington-Smythe had Made Out her Claim. Miss Smythe-Bilkington-Smythe thereupon Descended from the Remote Gallery in which she had been Quietly Sitting (in Obedience to the Instructions of the Highly Competent Solicitor) to Receive the Congratulations of her Friends. The New Baroness De Montazure and Front-de-Bœuf was Both Stout and Plain. The Highly Competent Solicitor Warmly Thanked the Sweet Young Lady (who was in Fact his Stenographer) for her Invaluable Services, and Raised her Salary on the Spot to 3*l*. 10*s*. a week.

Moral.—*Have the Client in Court.*

MR. JUSTICE HEAVYSIDE AND THE FAITHFUL
CLERK

MR. JUSTICE HEAVYSIDE AND THE
FAITHFUL CLERK

∽

SIR EBENEZER HEAVYSIDE was a Judge of
the High Court of Justice. He had been Ele-
vated to the Bench with the Full Approval of the
Profession. Nor were his Many Admirers Dis-
appointed by his Performances in the Judgment-Seat.
Indeed, it was Clear to All that (if Merit were the
Qualifying Test) Mr. Justice Heavyside would
Shortly be Promoted to the Court of Appeal or the
House of Lords. Heavyside, J., was Gratified that he
Stood so High in Public Estimation; but he had One
Abiding Sorrow. He Suffered Severely from a
Faithful but Incompetent Clerk. Man and Boy, the
Faithful Clerk had been with Mr. Justice Heavyside
for Forty Years. Day by Day his Imbecility Appeared
to Increase; yet his Employer had Never Summoned
Up Courage to Dismiss him. It was when Heavy-
side, J., Travelled on Circuit that the Doings of the
Faithful Clerk became Particularly Infuriating. The
Faithful Clerk could never Remember at what Hour
the Train Started, and he was Liable to Confuse St.
Pancras with Waterloo and Euston with Paddington.
Also he Made it a Practice to Lose the Tickets and
Leave the Depositions Behind. Here you Observe
Heavyside, J., and the Faithful Clerk on the Platform.
Once More the Faithful Clerk has Made a Mess of it.
They have Just Missed the Train. Mr. Justice

Heavyside will Arrive at Bodmin Two Hours Late for Dinner and he is Furious. Heavyside, J., is Wearing a Bowler, and the Faithful Clerk is the Gentleman in the Silk Hat.

Moral.—*Appearances are Deceptive.*

THE ESTABLISHED JUNIOR WHO HAD NOTHING
TO COMPLAIN OF

THE ESTABLISHED JUNIOR WHO HAD
NOTHING TO COMPLAIN OF

∽

AN Established Junior having Dined Comfort-
ably in his Flat Proceeded to Compare the
Present with the Past. Thirty Years Ago, the
Established Junior Reflected, he had Lived Laborious
Days. He had Devilled, Reported, Coached Colour-
ed Pupils, Written for the Papers, Compiled Legal
Treatises, and Perspired in County Courts. Then, at
Long Last, he had Turned the Corner. His Cases
had Become Heavy and Numerous. Whereas in his
Youth he had been Poorly Paid for his Eloquence in
Courts of Inferior Jurisdiction, he was now Richly
Rewarded for Sitting Silent behind Eminent Leaders
in the Higher Tribunals. Instead of Mugging Up his
Cases himself, he Allowed a Highly Intelligent Fellow
of All Saints' to Do that Disagreeable Job for him.
That Afternoon, the Established Junior Recalled with
Satisfaction, he had Attended a Consultation with an
Ex-Law Officer. After Twice Remarking "Quite,"
he had Left for Another Consultation with Another
Great Man, at which he Looked Important and Said
Nothing. It Comforted him to Think that he would
be Unable to be Present at the Hearing of Either
Matter, as he would be Very Busy Elsewhere, and
that his Absence would Only be Regarded by his
Client as Evidence of his Worth. The Established
Junior Felt that, on the whole, he had Nothing to

Complain of.   After All, there was Something to be Said for the Profession.   The Established Junior had Another Go of Pre-War Whisky, Lit a Second Corona, and Resumed his Agreeable Meditations.

Moral.—*Stick to a Stuff-Gown.*

THE DOMESTIC TYRANT, THE CRUSHED WORM,
AND THE BIBULOUS BUTLER

THE DOMESTIC TYRANT, THE CRUSHED
WORM, AND THE BIBULOUS BUTLER

◡◠

MR. JUSTICE CRASHER was a Profound
Lawyer, a Married Man, and a Domestic
Tyrant. Lady Crasher, after Filling the Rôle
of Crushed Worm for some Forty Years, Resolved to
Strike a Blow for Freedom. Her Chance soon Came.
One Monday Morning, after Crasher, J., had Left for
the Royal Courts of Justice, an Inspector of Police
Informed her Ladyship that her Butler, being at the
time Intoxicated, had Pledged with a Neighbouring
Pawnbroker a Silver Teapot and other Articles
Bearing the Crasher Crest. The Same Evening Lady
Crasher Mentioned to her Lord and Master that she
had Dismissed the Butler Without Notice, or Wages
in Lieu thereof, for Drunkenness and Dishonesty.
Crasher, J., Exhibited Violent Displeasure, and
Pointed Out that the Butler would Certainly Bring an
Action for Wrongful Dismissal. Lady Crasher
Listened Unmoved, and did not Disclose the Strength
of her Hand. When on Tuesday Morning a Dingy
Person Served a Writ upon Lady Crasher in a Suit
entitled "Binns *v.* Crasher (Married Woman)" Mr.
Justice Crasher Screamed with Passion and Insisted
that the Matter must be Settled Forthwith. Lady
Crasher's Quiet Reply that she would not Pay the
Disgusting Wretch a Farthing and that she would
Fight the Case in Person Caused Crasher, J., to Use

Very Ungentlemanly Language. Lady Crasher Gathered from his Remarks that she had, amongst Other Notable Disadvantages, the Temperament of a Mule and the Intellect of a Child of Seven. The Day of Reckoning Arrived and Lady Crasher Appeared in Person. Was she Defeated? Far from it. Lady Crasher Cross-examined the Bibulous Butler Inside Out, and he Never had a Look-in. The Next Day the Newspapers of the Metropolis Rang with the Praises of Lady Crasher. The *Daily Howl* Contained her Portrait; the *Daily Screech* Called her "Portia Rediviva"; and the *Thunderer* had a Leader in which Lady Crasher was Thanked for the Splendid Stand she had made on behalf of the Employers of Domestic Servants. Mr. Justice Crasher took the Dignified Course of Never Alluding to the Victory which Lady Crasher had Won. But his Reign as a Domestic Tyrant was Over, and thereafter Crasher, J., Became a Considerate and Respectful Husband.

Moral.—*Fight.*

1898   1928

THE YOUTH WHO RESOLVED ALWAYS TO
MAKE A CAREFUL NOTE OF THE FACTS

THE YOUTH WHO RESOLVED ALWAYS TO MAKE A CAREFUL NOTE OF THE FACTS

∽

THERE was Once a Youth who was Instructed to Appear for the Crown in a Case at Quarter Sessions. Being both Industrious and Prudent the Youth Made a Careful Note from which to Open the Facts and the Law to the Jury. The Note in its Final Form was Completed at 2 a.m. on the Day Fixed for the Trial. The Youth Sat Up Late because he was Very Anxious that it should be both Full and Accurate. The Note (which was on Two Sheets of Paper United by a Fastener) was as follows:—

CHARGE ⎰ (a) Larceny of boots.
⎱ (b) Receiving same well knowing to be stolen.

N.B.—Onus on Crown; but *no reasonable doubt*.

FACTS: 6th October, 1897—10.15 a.m.

Prisoner seen near shop by
(1) J. Brown.
(2) J. Brown, jun.

Both struck by Prisoner's appearance.
(a) Black Eye.
(b) Limp.

Same Evening—11.45 p.m. (about)

☞ *Crash heard.*

J. Brown goes downstairs.

☞ *Sees Prisoner escaping from window.*

263

Next Day.
 Prisoner Arrested by P.C.
 N.B.—actually wearing boots.
 Statement to P.C.:
     "I done it."
 Submit onus discharged:
  (1) Wearing of boots.
  (2) Admission to P.C.

Shaking All Over the Youth Opened the Case. On the Whole it Went Very Well. There was an Awkward Pause at One Moment because the Youth Could not Read the Words "Crash Heard," but Ultimately the Mists Cleared Away, and he was Able to Resume his Interrupted Address.

Pleased with his Performance, the Youth Resolved that he would Never Go into Court without a Careful Note of the Facts and the Law.

Thirty Years Later the Youth (now a K.C.) had to Open a Running-Down Case. After a Short Chat with his Junior he Wrote on the Back of his Brief (which he had not Read) the words "How Much?" He then made a Fluent and Convincing Speech. In the Course of his Address he Referred to the Plaintiff More than Once as "this Poor Old Gentleman." The Plaintiff in Truth was an Elderly Widow. But this Little Misapprehension didn't Matter a Bit and he Got a Nice Verdict.

 Moral.—*Stick to Your Note.*

THE BEGINNER WHO THOUGHT HE WOULD
DO IT HIMSELF

THE BEGINNER WHO THOUGHT HE
WOULD DO IT HIMSELF

∽

A BEGINNER, in the Temporary Absence of his Leader, Found himself Opposed to a Big Pot in the Commercial Court. Though Greatly Alarmed, the Beginner Bore himself Bravely. To his Surprise and Delight the Beginner Managed to Cross-Examine the Big Pot's Principal Witness with Such Effect that he Needed a Good Deal of Rehabilitation. Rising to Re-Examine, the Big Pot Airily Observed to the Principal Witness: "I Suppose What You Meant by Your Last Answer was This," and Proceeded to Tell the Principal Witness Quite Clearly what he Meant. When the Beginner made a Dignified Protest the Judge Smilingly Suggested that the Big Pot might Shape his Question rather Differently. The Next Day the Beginner was in a County Court. The Plaintiff (for whom the Beginner Appeared) having Made an Awkward Admission to his Learned Friend on the Other Side, the Beginner Thought he would Employ the Excellent Formula of the Big Pot. He Did so. The Scene that Followed Beggars Description. The County Court Judge in a Voice of Thunder Ordered the Beginner to Sit Down. He then Rebuked the Beginner for his Gross Misconduct and Discussed the Question whether he would Commit him for Contempt, or Merely Report him to the General Council of the Bar. Finally he Expressed the Hope that the Incident would be a Lesson to the Beginner and Directed that the Case should be re-Heard on a Later Date before a Fresh Jury.

Moral.—*Wait till You're a Big Pot.*

THE CALLOW YOUTH, THE BRIEF IN THE
DIVORCE COURT, AND THE WEEPING LADY

THE CALLOW YOUTH, THE BRIEF IN
THE DIVORCE COURT, AND THE
WEEPING LADY

ᔕ

A CALLOW Youth Shortly After his Call Caused his Name to be Inscribed on the Roll of Counsel Desirous of Representing Poor Persons. He was Soon Rewarded with Instructions to Appear on behalf of a Female Petitioner in the Divorce Court. The Callow Youth Perused the Brief and Learned that the Female's Husband had been Going On Anyhow. Not Only had he Preferred the Society of Two Other Ladies to that of the Female Petitioner, but on various Occasions he had Treated her with Physical Violence. The Case, which was to be Tried on the Morrow, Appeared to be Plain Sailing. After Dining Quietly at "The Cock" the Callow Youth Returned to his Chambers to have a Final Look at the Brief. Turning Up the Light he Observed a Middle-Aged Lady Seated in the Arm-Chair. She Wore a Straw Boater and a Macintosh, and she was Weeping Quietly. The Callow Youth saw At Once what had Happened. It was Clear that his Client had Come for a Conference about the Case. Approaching the Arm-Chair the Callow Youth Begged the Weeping Lady to be Calm and Spoke a Few Tactful Words of Sympathy. The Weeping Lady with a Slight Hiccup Said Something about "a Couple." She then Sank into Complete

Unconsciousness. The Callow Youth Redoubled his Attentions and, Recalling the First Aid Lectures he had Once Attended, Did What he Deemed Necessary to Restore her to Life. As he was Engaged upon his Work of Mercy a Furious Cry Assailed his Ear. Turning Round, the Callow Youth Found himself in the Grasp of a Gigantic Male. While the Callow Youth was Staunching the Flow of Gore from his Injured Nose he Gathered that the Weeping Lady was the Laundress in charge of the Chambers; that she was Intoxicated, not for the First Time; and that her Husband (the Gigantic Male) had Come to Take her Home. The Callow Youth Retired to Rest a Poorer but a Wiser Man.

Moral.—*Don't Jump to Conclusions.*

THE CAREFUL LAWYER WHO COULD NOT
MAKE UP HIS MIND

THE CAREFUL LAWYER WHO COULD
NOT MAKE UP HIS MIND

∽

THERE was Once a Careful Lawyer who, as the Result of a Variety of Unexpected Circumstances, Found himself Elevated to the Bench. The Careful Lawyer was not Entirely Satisfied that he had the Necessary Qualifications for Judicial Office, and his Misgivings were Shared by those who Knew him Best. For, Most Unfortunately, he could not Make Up his Mind. In Chambers the Careful Lawyer Got on Well Enough by Affirming the Order of the Master and Directing that the Costs should be Costs in the Cause. And in Jury Cases the Careful Lawyer Discovered that it was not a Bad Plan to Read over the Evidence to the Jury and Ask them Such Questions as Counsel Suggested. But as a Rule the Careful Lawyer Found himself Sadly Puzzled. On Circuit he Spent Sleepless Nights Wondering whether the Prisoner ought to Have Two Months with Hard Labour or Three Months in the Second Division; and when he Tried a Non-Jury Case it was his Custom to Reserve his Judgment for so Long a Period of Time that he Often Forgot what the Case had been About. One Day, for a Change, they Put the Careful Lawyer in a Divisional Court. It was Hoped that he would Find the Job an Easy One. But the Careful Lawyer was so Bothered by Trying to Decide, whilst the Other Judgments were being

Delivered, whether he should Say that he Agreed with Them or that he Concurred with them, that he had a Nervous Breakdown from which he Never Recovered.

Moral.—*Toss Up.*

THE SILK WHO KNEW HOW TO MAKE A
GOOD SHOW

THE SILK WHO KNEW HOW TO MAKE
A GOOD SHOW

∽

THERE was Once a Plaintiff who Brought an Action in the Hope that the Defendant would Prefer not to Fight. But the Defendant Plucked Up Courage and Briefed a Silk whose Fame as a Cross-Examiner was World-Wide. As the Plaintiff, apart from being a Bad Egg in a General Way, had Spent Several Years in Penal Servitude, it was Clear that the Silk would have Some Material to Work Upon. A Week before the Case Came On the Silk Presided over a Consultation at which the Question of Evidence was Discussed. How was the Black Record of the Plaintiff to be Established? The Junior Suggested that the Certificate of his Conviction Duly Produced in Court would Suffice. The Silk Curtly Rejected this Proposal, and Gave Other Directions. When the Time Came for the Silk to Cross-Examine the Plaintiff the Court was Crowded with Expectant Members of the Public and Representatives of the Press. The Silk First Asked the Plaintiff whether he was in Good Health. Having Learned that the Plaintiff's Physical Condition was All that Could be Desired, the Silk Enquired where the Plaintiff Lived. After Ascertaining that he Resided in Tooting, the Silk Begged to be Informed Whether he Ever Went to the Country or the Sea-Side. If so, Which Place did he Like Best? The

Silk then Took the Plaintiff Through a Long List of Inland and Marine Health-Resorts and Gathered that he Usually Spent his Holidays at Margate. Did the Plaintiff Care, by any Chance, for Devonshire? What did he Think of the Moors of Devonshire? Did he Know them Well? Had he Found them Salubrious? Had he Found them So Salubrious that he had Lived on them for Seven Years? Did he Know the Stout Gentleman Standing Up at the Back of the Court? Was the Stout Gentleman a Warder at the Dartmoor Convict Establishment? Did he Know the Gentleman with a Broken Nose Standing Up in the Gallery? Was he a Fellow-Convict with the Plaintiff at the said Convict Establishment? Were the Plaintiff and the Gentleman with the Broken Nose Employed in the Quarries at the Same Time? When the Plaintiff had Given Satisfactory Answers to these Various Queries, the Silk Resumed his Seat. Was his Reputation as a Cross-Examiner Enhanced? It was. The Daily Journals Reported his Masterly Performance Word for Word, and the Public Wondered Once More at the Amazing Skill with which the Silk Managed to Worm the Truth out of a Cunning Scoundrel.

Moral.—*Do it in Style.*

MISS SNAFFLETON (INFANT) AND THE
OLD-FASHIONED JUDGE

MISS SNAFFLETON (INFANT)
AND
THE OLD-FASHIONED JUDGE

∽

THERE was Once a Judge of the Chancery
Division of the High Court of Justice who had
Old-Fashioned Views about Everything. In
Particular, about the Young. He did not Like the
Goings-On of the New Generation. Their Want of
Respect, their Indifference to the Conventions, their
Slangy Talk, and their Cocktail Parties were, in his
Opinion, Positively Intolerable. Therefore when the
Old-Fashioned Judge Received a Breezy and rather
Ungrammatical Letter from his Ward of Court, Miss
Snaffleton (Infant), Saying that she Wanted to See
him *At Once* about a Matter of *Urjent Importence*, he
Determined to Give her a Piece of his Mind. The
Old-Fashioned Judge had Already Informed Master
Pooter (who Took the S to Z Business) that he had
been Far too Indulgent to Miss Snaffleton (Infant) in
the Matter of Finance. The Following Monday Miss
Snaffleton Blew In. She was Costumed for the Game
of Golf and was Furnished with a Cigarette. Miss
Snaffleton (Infant) At Once Took Control of the
Situation. After Telling the Old-Fashioned Judge
that he Looked a Dear in those Funny Clothes, she
Said she was Sure he was Going to be Sweet. The
Fact was she Wanted to be Married. Tommy was
Absolutely It and the Poor Lamb had Quite Given

283

Up Lifting His Elbow. He had an Interest or Something in a Motor Business and was Doing Terribly Well, Would the Old-Fashioned Judge be an Absolute Angel and Give his Consent? Did the Old-Fashioned Judge Take a Firm Line ? He Did. The Old-Fashioned Judge Insisted that the Marriage should not Take Place till a Fortnight had Elapsed (in Order that Miss Snaffleton might be Sure she Knew her Own Mind) and Declined to Allow her More than 3,000*l.* a year Until she had Satisfied him that this Amount was Insufficient for her and Tommy's Requirements. He also Agreed to Buy One of Tommy's Cars and to Give Miss Snaffleton (Infant) Away at the Hymeneal Altar.

Moral.—*Be Firm.*

MRS. SARAH STOUT, THE LAST WILL OF
MR. BUFFIN, AND THE DRAFT AFFIDAVIT

MRS. SARAH STOUT, THE LAST WILL OF MR. BUFFIN, AND THE DRAFT AFFIDAVIT

∽

WHEN Mr. Buffin, of 1, Plum Tree Court, Temple, E.C.4, Passed Away in his Eighty-Ninth Year, his Last Will and Testament could not be Discovered. This Circumstance Annoyed his Nephews and Nieces Greatly; for Mr. Buffin was a Bachelor and the Nephews and Nieces had Expectations. And when, as the Result of a Diligent Search in a Glory-Hole Containing the Rubbish of Years, Mrs. Sarah Stout, the Laundress, Unearthed the Missing Document, the Anxieties of the Nephews and Nieces were not at an End. For, Owing to the Attentions of a Mouse with a Morbid Appetite, the Name of the Second Attesting Witness had Disappeared, and the First Attesting Witness was Dead. What was to be Done? Mrs. Sarah Stout again Came to the Rescue, for she Well Remembered about Three Years ago Poor Mr. Buffin Saying Would she Come and Sign her Name Here Next his Clerk's Name, which the Clerk he Signed it Too the Same as What Mrs. Sarah Stout did, and it was a Damp, Foggy Day, and she Noticed Poor Mr. Buffin had a Nasty Cough and she Said to Herself, she Said, Well, she Said, she Hoped Mr. Buffin wasn't Really Ill, and he Got through the Winter Nicely After All, and that Poor Clerk he was the First to Go, and a Pleasant

Man he was, though a Little Too Fond of a Quick One. While Mrs. Stout was Telling this Tale, the Solicitor in Charge of Mr. Buffin's Affairs was Making a Careful Note of her Observations. In Due Course Mrs. Stout Received the Affidavit which she was to Swear. In Successive Paragraphs it Related that Mrs. Stout had Long been Acquainted with the Testator and his Clerk; that She Well Remembered the 4th November, 1927, as the Weather was Peculiarly Inclement; that on that Date the Testator Requested her to Witness his Last Will and Testament; that the Testator also Informed her that his said Clerk would be the First Attesting Witness; that she had thereupon Signed her Name in the Presence of the Testator and of his said Clerk, and that his said Clerk had Likewise Signed his Name in the Presence of Herself and of the Testator; that she Recognised the Document (now Produced to her and Marked " S.S.1.") as a Copy of the Document which she had so Signed together with the said Clerk of the Testator; that the Testator to the Best of her Belief was on the said Date of Sound Mind and of Testamentary Capacity; and that she was Informed and Believed that the said Clerk of the Testator was now Deceased. Mrs. Sarah Stout was so Delighted by the Purity of her Language and the Perfection of her Style that she forthwith made up her Mind to Adopt a Literary Career.

Moral.—*Magna est Veritas.*

THE KINDLY JUDGE AND LITTLE EFFIE

THE KINDLY JUDGE AND LITTLE EFFIE

∾

A KINDLY Judge (of the Chancery Division) Found himself Confronted by a Difficult Problem. Was Little Effie (a Ward of Court) to go to School, or Not?

Counsel Representing Little Effie's Grandmother Contended that Little Effie, by Reason of her Nervous Temperament, was not Fitted for Contact with the Rough Companions whom she would Doubtless Encounter at the Proposed Educational Establishment.

The Advocate Voicing the Opinions of the Maiden Aunt Took the Line that Little Effie was a Perfectly Normal and Healthy Child who would Derive Immense Benefit from the Discipline and Gaiety of School Life.

The Kindly Judge Wisely Suggested that before Reading the Affidavits he should Interview Little Effie in his Private Room.

When Little Effie Presented herself the Kindly Judge (who was a Family Man) Found himself Attracted by her Cropped Head and her large Blue Eyes. To Put Little Effie Completely at her Ease the Kindly Judge Invited her to Try on his Wig and to Observe the Effect in his Looking-Glass. After a Pleasant Little Chat the Kindly Judge Resumed his Wig and Returned to Court. Counsel Thereupon Set to Work.

"A Month Ago," ran Paragraph One of the Grandmother's Affidavit, "Effie Suffered from a Bad Attack of Ring-Worm and her Head had to be Shaved." The Kindly Judge forthwith Adjourned the Proceedings *Sine Die*, and Sent his Clerk Out for a Bottle (Large Size) of Condy's Fluid.

Moral.—*Read the Affidavits First.*

MR. BOBBY CHUMP, THE SUCCESSFUL
DEFENCE AND ITS SINGULAR CONSE-
QUENCES

MR. BOBBY CHUMP, THE SUCCESS-FUL DEFENCE AND ITS SINGULAR CONSEQUENCES

∽

MRS. BOBBY CHUMP was Greatly Pleased when the Judge at the Old Bailey Asked her Bobby to Defend a Prisoner. Her Pleasure was all the Greater when Bobby Telephoned to Say that the Prisoner had been Acquitted, and that the Judge had Invited Him to Dinner. He did not Add that the Jury had Stopped the Case before Bobby had Cross-examined Anybody or Delivered the Eloquent Speech which he and Mrs. Chump had Prepared in Consultation.

When Bobby Returned to the Flat at Midnight Mrs. Bobby was greatly Alarmed by his Manner and Appearance. Something had Happened. Bobby's Gait was Unsteady; his Words, which were Imperfectly Formed, Came in Strange Sequence; and he had a Fixed and Feeble Smile. It was Clear to Mrs. Bobby that he Must be Got to Bed at Once.

The Next Day Bobby was Very Much Better. And to Mrs. Bobby's Great Relief, Bobby was Able to Assure Her at Breakfast that his Experience of the Night Before was Not Uncommon at the Bar. Advocacy, he Explained, Exposes the Nervous System to a Tremendous Strain. Some Speakers Suffer before, Some after, the Making of the Oratorical Effort. Bobby, she Gathered, Belonged to the Latter Class; Brougham, Russell, and Birkenhead to the Former.

Moral.—*Take Sanatogen.*

295

THE PROFOUND LAWYER WHO RECEIVED
A SUBPŒNA *AD TESTIFICANDUM*

THE PROFOUND LAWYER WHO
RECEIVED A SUBPŒNA *AD*
TESTIFICANDUM

∽

A PROFOUND Lawyer, Whose Fame as an Orator and a Cross-Examiner was of the World-Wide Order, once Chanced to Observe a Collision between a Taxi-Cab and a Bus. When a Stout and Peremptory Policeman Demanded his Name and Address the Profound Lawyer Gladly Gave the Desired Particulars. He was Well Pleased to Have an Opportunity of Entering the Witness-Box and Showing Everybody how Evidence Ought to be Given. A Month Later the Profound Lawyer was Visited by a Managing Clerk of Unprepossessing Appearance and Considerable Intelligence. Invited by his Visitor to Give a Proof, the Profound Lawyer Proceeded to Dictate an Accurate Account of the Disaster, Prudently Retaining a Copy of the Resultant Document so that he might from Time to Time Refresh his Memory before the Hearing of the Cause. In Due Course the Profound Lawyer Received a Subpœna Requiring him to Testify on behalf of the Plaintiff in the King's Bench Division of the High Court of Justice.

Was the Evidence of the Profound Lawyer a Success? Far from it.

When the Profound Lawyer was Asked to Mention the Date of the Accident he was Quite Unable to

Remember it. So Confidential were the Tones in which he Began his Story that the Judge Sharply Ordered Him to Speak Up. When the Plan was Handed to the Profound Lawyer he Held it Upside Down. Twice he Endeavoured to Tell the Court what he had Said to his Wife when he Got Home in the Evening. His Reservations and Qualifications were so Abundant that it Appeared Doubtful Whether he had seen Anything at All. A Short Cross-Examination Elicited the Fact that he had Learnt his Proof by Heart. In his Summing-Up the Judge Told the Jury to Dismiss from their Minds the Evidence of the Profound Lawyer, as it was Entirely Worthless.

Moral.—*Look the Other Way.*

THE HIGH SHERIFF'S CHAPLAIN AND THE
ASSIZE SERMON WHICH GAVE UNIVERSAL
SATISFACTION

THE HIGH SHERIFF'S CHAPLAIN
AND THE ASSIZE SERMON WHICH
GAVE UNIVERSAL SATISFACTION

∽

A HIGH Sheriff's Chaplain, whose Sermons on Various Occasions were Greatly Admired, Determined that when he Preached before the Judge of Assize his Lordship should not be Disappointed. He accordingly Composed with the Utmost Care a Dignified Dissertation in which Scholarship, Dogma, and Respect for the Judicial Office were Suitably Blended. In Due Course the High Sheriff's Chaplain Climbed into the Pulpit, and the Judge of Assize, with a Sinking Heart, Prepared for the Worst.

When he Opened his Manuscript the High Sheriff's Chaplain had the Shock of His Life. He Realised with Horror that his Wife had Furnished him with an Address which he had Intended for the Annual Parochial Outing of the Boy Scouts and Girl Guides. There was Only One Thing to be Done. The High Sheriff's Chaplain Mumbled through the First Page, which Dealt with the Evils of Cigarette Smoking (Boy Scouts) and the Evils of Gossip (Girl Guides), and Tottered into the Vestry. The Whole Thing was Over in Three Minutes.

Was the Sermon a Success? It was. The Same Evening the Judge of Assize Told the High Sheriff's Chaplain at the Bishop's Dinner-Table that he had

Never Enjoyed a Sermon so Much, and that he Should Certainly Mention the Name of the High Sheriff's Chaplain to the Prime Minister in Connection with the Vacant Deanery of Porchester.

Moral.—*It Doesn't Matter*.

THE BRILLIANT PERSON, THE VULGAR IN-
DIVIDUAL WITH A COCKNEY ACCENT AND
THE TWO MALEFACTORS

THE BRILLIANT PERSON, THE VULGAR INDIVIDUAL WITH A COCKNEY ACCENT AND THE TWO MALEFACTORS

∽

T HERE was Once a Brilliant Person who Regretted the Decay of Eloquence at the Bar. He had Studied the Subject of Rhetoric and was Himself a Splendid Performer. The Brilliant Person Knew all about Proem, Narrative, Arguments and Peroration; furthermore, he was both Skilled in the Use of Metaphor and a Master of Expression. So far as Style was Concerned the Brilliant Person Preferred Lysias to Antiphon.

The Brilliant Person (whose Practice was on the Small Side) Felt that His Chance had Come when he was Briefed to Defend One of Two Alleged Malefactors. He Determined that he would Show those Duds at the Old Bailey how to Do the Trick.

The Malefactors were Charged with Receiving Goods Well Knowing them to have been Stolen. The Brilliant Person Learned that Malefactor Number Two was to be Represented by a Vulgar Individual with a Cockney Accent. This Annoyed the Brilliant Person a Good Deal, for it was Clear to him that, while his Own Client was Certain of Acquittal, the Case of Number Two Needed Delicate Handling. It was a Pity, the Brilliant Person Reflected, that the

Destinies of Both Prisoners had not been Entrusted to him.   The Case Came on.

The Brilliant Person Made a Masterly Speech in which he Expounded the Law, Analysed the Evidence, and Explained to the Jury the Vital Distinction between Actual and Constructive Notice.   In his Concluding Sentences the Brilliant Person Invoked the Spirit of Justice.   He also Called Three Witnesses to Character.

The Vulgar Individual Began his Observations by Wishing the Jury a Happy New Year.   He then Told them a Story about a Scotchman and a Jew. During the Course of his Rollicking Address, which Filled the Brilliant Person with Shame, the Vulgar Individual made no Attempt to Grapp ℈ with the Difficulties of the Case.   Nor (inasmu h as the Second Malefactor had been Repeatedly Convicted) did he Call any Witnesses to Character.

But, to the Unspeakable Fury of the Brilliant Person, the Jury, without Leaving the Box, Convicted the Brilliant Person's Client and Acquitted Number Two.

Moral.—*Acquire a Cockney Accent.*

LORD PUSHLEIGH OF RUNNYMEDE AND
HIS COAT-OF-ARMS

LORD PUSHLEIGH OF RUNNYMEDE
AND HIS COAT-OF-ARMS

MR. SAMUEL PUSHLEIGH, having been Called to the Bar, Quickly Realised that if he was to Get to the Top he must Take Part in Political Life. So Mr. Pushleigh Became a Friend of the Downtrodden and Oppressed and Joined the Forward Party. He had a Bust of Danton on his Book Case; he Laughed Hoarsely when the House of Lords was Mentioned; and he Spoke on Countless Platforms in a Loud Tone of Voice in Favour of Votes for Minors, the Destruction of Capitalism, a Single Chamber, the Abolition of the Army and the Navy, and the Nationalisation of Everything that was Left Over.

Thirty Years later Mr. (now Sir) Samuel Pushleigh, K.C., Reached the Zenith of his Career. When Title and Coat-of-Arms had to be Decided Upon, Sir Samuel Pushleigh Recalled that an Ancestor (Maternal) was Believed to have Fought by the Side of the Black Prince. His Suggestion that he should be the First Baron Crécy of Poictiers was, to his Annoyance, Rejected by the Authorities, and Ultimately he was Gazetted as Lord Pushleigh of Runnymede. But the Coat-of-Arms, which Arrived with the Coronet and Robes, was All that Lord Pushleigh Could Desire. The Crest (a Crowned Cross-Bow, *Gules*) Surmounted a Shield on which were Quartered First, Three

Leopards of England, Proper, Charged with the Fleurs-de-Lys of France, *Argent*, Secondly, Two Bowmen, Mourant, *Sable*, on a Chevron *Topaz*, between Three Arrow-Heads in Pale. Emblematical Figures Representing Truth and Justice were the Supporters. On a Label beneath Ran the Proud Motto: *Pour Roy et Loy.*

Moral.—*Why not?*

THE JUDICIAL PERSONAGE WHO DISAPPROVED
OF CINEMAS AND SENSATIONAL LITERATURE

THE JUDICIAL PERSONAGE WHO
DISAPPROVED OF CINEMAS AND
SENSATIONAL LITERATURE

∽

A JUDICIAL Personage of Ripe Experience Held Decided Views on the Subject of Cinemas and Sensational Literature. He Felt that they were the Main Causes of the Demoralisation of the Working Classes, the State of Unrest in India, and the General Decadence of the Present Generation. Whenever a Suitable Opportunity Presented itself the Judicial Personage Let Fly at Both of these Weapons of the Evil One. If Informed by the Police Officer in Charge of the Case that the Oaf or Flapper in the Dock had been a Constant Attendant at the Flicks or a Regular Reader of Detective Tales the Judicial Personage Preached an Impressive Sermon and Gave the Offender not Less than Nine Months. And when Responding at a Public Dinner for the Bench, the Guests of the Evening, or What Not, the Judicial Personage did not Fail to Say a Few Forcible Words on Each of these Topics.

Though, Greatly to his Disappointment, his Sermons Seemed to Fall upon Deaf Ears, the Judicial Personage Manfully Continued to Sow the Good Seed.

Once a Week (on Saturday Afternoons) the Judicial Personage Allowed himself a Little Relaxation. He Lunched at the Megatherium, Took a Two-and-

Fourpenny Seat at Whatever Cinema the Hall-Porter Recommended, and Returned to his Club to Tea. During the Latter Refection he Read the Last Edgar Wallace.

Moral.—*Quite Right Too.*

THE FIERCE ADVOCATE WHO REALLY HAD
A SOFT HEART

THE FIERCE ADVOCATE WHO
REALLY HAD A SOFT HEART

⌒

THERE was Once a Fierce Advocate Who Carried All before him. He was Very Alarming in Court. When he Opened the Case for the Plaintiff or the Defendant his Eye Flashed, and he Said Such Nasty and Sarcastic Things about the Other Side that the Jury were Quite Anxious to Give him a Verdict Then and There. While the Fierce Advocate's Eye was Flashing and he was Saying the Nasty and Sarcastic Things, the Other Side Did its Best to Look Unconcerned.

When it was his Turn to Cross-Examine, The Fierce Advocate Usually Began by Asking the Witness a Few Simple and Direct Questions—whether he was not a Dirty Dog, or a Swindling Scoundrel, or Something of that Sort—and then he Took the Witness through the Details of his Discreditable Past. Company Promoters and Money Lenders Shook in Their Shoes when the Fierce Advocate Got Going, and Experienced Leading Ladies Tottered in a Fainting Condition from the Box. Only the Most Courageous of the Judges Ventured to Criticize his Methods, for it was Well Known that the Fierce Advocate Enjoyed a Breeze with the Bench.

Did the Fierce Advocate Behave in Like Fashion in Private Life? He did not. The Fierce Advocate had Lived in the Same Uncomfortable Rooms for

Thirty Years because he was Afraid to Tell the Proprietor he Wanted to Go Away. His Companions were two Canaries, three Cats and a Parrot, to which Birds and Beasts he was Devotedly Attached. And the Fierce Advocate's Favourite Bed-Side Books were "Jessica's First Prayer" and "Froggy's Little Brother," with one of which he Cried himself to Sleep Every Night.

Moral.—*Be Fierce.*

THE BRILLIANT ORATOR WHO WON FAME
AS A DEFENDER

THE BRILLIANT ORATOR WHO WON
FAME AS A DEFENDER

∽

A BRILLIANT Orator once Shot like a Comet across the Legal Firmament. His More Obvious Endowments were a Commanding Presence, a Rich Voice and a Piercing Eye. The Brilliant Orator's Law was a little Shaky, but he Made Up for This by Knowing All about Everything Else. As a Defender of Important Criminals the Brilliant Orator was Admitted to be *Facile Princeps*. No Murder Case was Complete Without Him. The News that the Police had Arrested the Suspected Person and that the Brilliant Orator had been Retained for the Defence would Appear Simultaneously in the Evening Papers.

At or about the Same Time Enterprising Publishers would Purchase the Serial and Other Rights in the Autobiography of the Suspected Person. The Common Form of Agreement Required that the Suspected Person should Furnish the Completed Manuscript within Three Days after the Conclusion of the Proceedings, and that the Proceedings should be Deemed to be Concluded on the Dismissal of the Suspected Person's Appeal (if any) by the Court of Criminal Appeal. The Brilliant Orator's Favourite Line was that the Murdered Individual was an Undesirable Citizen who had Got no more than his Deserts, but that the Suspected Person had, in fact,

Fired the Revolver by Accident, or Picked Up the Wrong Bottle in the Dark.

When the Suspected Person was a Female of Agreeable Appearance this Defence Went Off very Well indeed.

It was in his Perorations that the Brilliant Orator was Heard at his Best. After Reminding the Jury that the Chain of Evidence was as Strong as the Weakest Link in it, that it was for the Crown to Establish the Case against the Prisoner beyond the Scintilla of a Reasonable Doubt, and that the Doctor who had Conducted the Post-Mortem Examination had Very Fairly Said that he could not Swear that the Murdered Individual was not a Man of Violent Temper, the Brilliant Orator, in a Final Crash of Eloquence, would Ask them to Remember that it was Better that Ninety-nine Innocent Persons should be Convicted than that One Guilty Person should be Acquitted. The Jury, however, always Understood what he Meant. At the Close of his Address the Brilliant Orator would Sink into his Seat in a State of Collapse. There were Cavillers who said that the Brilliant Orator had Secured the Conviction of Several of his Clients; but the Public Knew Better.

Moral.—*Perorate*.

DIEHARD AND STICKIT, JJ.

DIEHARD AND STICKIT, JJ.

EARLY in the Nineteenth Century Young Mr. Diehard and Young Mr. Stickit, Barristers-at-Law, Observed with Concern that the then Members of the Judiciary Exhibited a Tendency to Cling to Office Long After the Process of Physical and Mental Decay had Set In. Mr. Diehard and Mr. Stickit Regretted on Public Grounds both the Incompetence and the Immortality of these Judicial Limpets.

Years Rolled by, and Mr. Diehard and Mr. Stickit, now of Middle Age, Received the Reward of Merit and Took their Seats upon the Bench. More Years Rolled by, and Diehard, J., and Stickit, J., Began to Note that Youthful Counsel would not Speak Up, that Leaders Insisted on Mumbling, and that the Bar was Deteriorating Day by Day.

When Ninety-Three and Ninety-Four Respectively, Diehard and Stickit, JJ., were Still Going Strong. They often Assured Each Other that they were Best Serving the Interests of the Country by Holding on to their Jobs; that of all Judicial Qualifications Ripe Experience was the Most Precious; and that if they were to Retire the Lord Chancellor would Look In Vain for Anybody who was Fit to Succeed Either of Them.

Moral.—*Don't Desert the Gold Standard.*

MR. BLUEBAG, MR. BERT BAUMSTEIN AND
"THE OLD JUDGE"

MR. BLUEBAG, MR. BERT BAUMSTEIN
AND "THE OLD JUDGE"

∽

M R. BLUEBAG having Ample Leisure after his Call to the Bar Took to Visiting the Pictures. Sickened by the Foolishness of the Plots Unfolded before him, Mr. Bluebag Took Pen in Hand to See whether he could Emulate the Imbecility of their Authors. The result was Excellent.

Mr. Bluebag's Film Began with the Old Judge, Fully Robed, Returning on Christmas Eve to his Chambers in Pump Court, after a Hard Day's Work. It was Snowing. To the Old Judge's Amazement he Found a Newly-Born Infant (Female) on the Doorstep. Wrapping the Infant Tenderly in his Full-Bottomed Wig, the Old Judge Carried her to the Fire-Side, where, with the Help of his Old Clerk (with White Hair), he Bathed and Fed her.

As the Infant had Brought a New Joy into his Life —for he was Lonely—he Adopted her.

When a Beautiful Young Woman of Eighteen the Infant Produced a Sealed Letter which she had Always Worn Round her Neck. It Informed the Old Judge that she was the Child of his Son, who had been Shipped in Disgrace to the Antipodes and Never Heard of Again.

On the Nineteenth Anniversary of her Discovery on the Doorstep, an Exhausted and Dying Woman

Knocked at the Old Judge's Door. She was Covered with Snow, for it was Snowing. In Faltering Accents she Confessed that the Infant was no Relation of the Old Judge, but her Own Deserted Child. She then Passed Away in the Old Judge's Arms. Was the Old Judge Distressed by her News? No. He had Lost a Grand-Daughter, but he had Won a Bride. And on the Next Christmas Eve there was a Wedding (in the Snow) of Surpassing Splendour at Westminster Abbey, Attended by the Lord Chancellor, the Lords of Appeal, the Lords Justices, the Judges of the High Court, the County Court Judges, and the Three Official Referees. Throughout the Performance (Ran the Instructions of Mr. Bluebag) "Goodnight, Sweetheart" and "Always" were to be Played upon a Mechanical Organ.

Hardly had Mr. Bluebag Completed the Manuscript when Mr. Bert Baumstein, of The Universal Amalgamated Flicks Inc., was Ushered in. He Wished to Consult Mr. Bluebag on the Subject of a Broken Contract. While he was Perusing the Contract Mr. Bluebag was Startled by the Sound of Muffled Sobs. Looking Up, he Observed Mr. Baumstein Quietly Weeping over "The Old Judge." Mastering his Emotion, Mr. Baumstein Enquired whether Mr. Bluebag was Free to Dispose of the Performing Rights in the most Human, Inspiring, Touching and Elevating Scenario he had ever Read. If he were a Willing Vendor Mr. Baumstein could offer Fifty Thousand Pounds (Spot Cash) and a Ten per cent. Royalty. Mr. Bluebag Closed. "The Old Judge" has had a Phenomenal Run in London, New

York, Rome, Paris, Vienna, Budapest, Constanti-
nople and Leningrad, and will shortly be Generally
Released.   Mr. Bluebag has Retired from the Bar.

Moral.—*Go to the Flicks.*

MR. POTTLE'S NASTY ACCIDENT, THE
SAGACIOUS COOK, AND THE ACTION AT LAW

MR. POTTLE'S NASTY ACCIDENT, THE SAGACIOUS COOK, AND THE ACTION AT LAW

∽

WHEN Mr. Pottle was Beginning to Recover from his Nasty Accident on the Escalator he Very Properly Consulted his Lawyer. The Opinion of Eminent Counsel was Taken, and Mr. Pottle was Assured that if he were to Issue a Writ his Prospects of Success were Good. The Underlying Note of the Opinion was that the Escalator was in the Nature of a Trap, and that Mr. Pottle had not been Given Sufficient Warning of its Dangerous Qualities, whether by the Railway Company or its Servants and Agents.

When Mr. Pottle's Sagacious Cook Came to Take the Orders for the Day, Mr. Pottle Told her of the Encouraging Advice he had Received and Invited her Views. The Sagacious Cook Replied that, for her Part, she would have Nothing to do with those Lawyers who would Go and Say that the Notice Said You were to Step Off with Your Right Foot; that she was Sure Mr. Pottle had Stepped Off with his Left Foot; and that it had All Happened (if Mr. Pottle didn't Mind her Saying so) because Mr. Pottle had Left his Spectacles at Home. Mr. Pottle Smiled Kindly at the Simplicity of the Sagacious Cook.

Twelve Months having Elapsed the Action Came

on for Hearing, and Mr. Pottle Recovered Heavy Damages.

Fifteen Months later a New Trial was Ordered as the Judge had Misdirected the Jury on the Law relating to Invitees and Licensees.

Two Years having Rolled by, a Second Judgment in Mr. Pottle's Favour was Upheld by a Majority in the Court of Appeal. Three Years afterwards the House of Lords Reversed it by a Majority of One.

In the Speech of the Lord Chancellor it was Pointed Out that a Notice Exhibited at the Foot of Escalator Warned Passengers to Step Off with the Right Foot; that the Evidence Clearly Established that Mr. Pottle had Stepped Off with his Left Foot; and that if Mr. Pottle had not Unfortunately Left his Spectacles at Home the Accident would not have Happened.

Moral.—*Ring the Bell.*

THE CHANCERY JUDGE WHO OBSERVED
THAT THE INTELLECT OF HIS COMMON-
LAW BROTHER WAS FAILING

THE CHANCERY JUDGE WHO
OBSERVED THAT THE INTELLECT
OF HIS COMMON-LAW BROTHER
WAS FAILING

∽

ONE Day a Chancery Judge Met a Common-Law Brother in the Judge's Corridor as the Latter was Hurrying towards the Luncheon Room. Full of the Interesting Point which was being Developed in His Court, the Chancery Judge Stopped his Common-Law Brother so that he might Secure the Benefit of his Opinion. Button-holing his Colleague, the Chancery Judge Explained that the Main Question was whether the Appointment of the Land to Trustees for Sale was Good. This Depended upon whether the Will of the Testator had Effected a Conversion of the Land into Personalty. The Underlying Difficulty of the Matter, he said, was Due to an *Obiter Dictum* of Mr. Justice Cockwitch in an Unreported Case which Seemed to Throw an Entirely Fresh Light on the Statute of Uses. The Chancery Judge Observed, as his Narrative Proceeded, that his Common-Law Brother Seemed both Listless and Apathetic. And when the Chancery Judge Asked his Common-Law Brother what he Thought about the Problem and his Common-Law Brother Replied, "The Answer is a Lemon," the Chancery Judge was Reluctantly Driven to the Conclusion that the Intellect of his Common-Law Brother was Failing.

Moral.—*Read Snell.*

335

THE HUSBANDS WHO MET IN THE
ELYSIAN FIELDS

THE HUSBANDS WHO MET IN THE
ELYSIAN FIELDS

〜

MEETING in the Elysian Fields, Two Husbands Proceeded to Exchange their Melancholy Experiences in the Divorce Court. Eighteen-Hundred-and-Sixty was Happily Married, but One Fine Day he Accompanied a Lady from Hyde Park to the Recently-Opened Railroad Terminus at New Cross in a Four-Wheeled Cab. His Wife, Hearing of the Incident, Presented a Petition in the Divorce Court. The Judge Promptly Decided that Opportunity for Misconduct having been Afforded by the Expedition in the Four-Wheeled Cab, there was a Presumption that Eighteen-Hundred-and-Sixty had been Unfaithful to his Marriage Vow. Thus his Home had been Broken Up.

Nineteen-Hundred-and-Thirty said that he had no Such Luck. Desiring the Dissolution of his Marriage (for his Wife was both Ill-Tempered and Plain) he Visited the Hotel Magnifique, Shrimpton-on-Sea, with a Sympathetic Companion. They had not been Formally Introduced. Their Room was Number 27. Tea was Brought to them in the Morning by the Chambermaid. The Judge Decided without Hesitation that in all the Circumstances there was no Satisfactory Evidence of Matrimonial Misconduct on the Part of Nineteen-Hundred-and-Thirty. In Fact, the Presumption was that it was a Put-Up Job. Eighteen-

Hundred-and-Sixty Opined that Times had Changed Since his Day and Suggested that they should Have a Little Refreshment at the Adjacent Bar. Nineteen-Hundred-and-Thirty Agreed with Alacrity.

Moral.—*Omnia Præsumuntur*.

THE ERUDITE JUDGE AND THE QUESTION
OF DOUBTFUL ADMISSIBILITY

340

THE ERUDITE JUDGE AND THE
QUESTION OF DOUBTFUL
ADMISSIBILITY

೧

THERE Lived in the Past an Erudite Judge who
Considered that he was Rather Hot Stuff.
Nor was his Good Opinion of himself without
Justification; for he had the Law at his Finger Ends
and he Expounded it in Language which was both
Elegant and Precise. When Opportunity Offered the
Erudite Judge would Enrich the Law Reports with a
Judgment in which he Discussed all the Authorities,
Exposed the Fallacies of Deceased Members of the
Bench, Corrected the Errors of Legal Writers, and
Generally Cleared Things Up for Posterity. One
Fine Day, while the Erudite Judge was Trying a Case
in the Common Jury List, Counsel for the Plaintiff
Asked the Witness What the Charwoman had Said
when the Witness Told her that the Plaintiff had
Fallen Over the Pail on the Stairs. The Erudite
Judge Directed the Witness not to Answer the Ques-
tion, and Ordered the Jury to Withdraw. After a
Protracted Argument as to the Admissibility of the
Question the Erudite Judge Adjourned the Hearing
so that he might Consider the Matter Fully.

The Next Day the Erudite Judge Loosed Off a
Splendid Bit of Work. No Aspect of the Law of
Evidence was Left Untouched. Beginning with the
Pandects of Justinian, the Erudite Judge Took his

Hearers through the Canon Law and the Year-Books, and thus Traced to its Source the Doctrine of the Inadmissibility of Hearsay Evidence. By Eleven Forty-Five the Erudite Judge had Got to *Whitelocke* v. *Baker* (13 Ves. 514), Declarations by Deceased Persons, Inscriptions on Tombstones, and the Facts Properly to be Regarded as *Res Gestæ*. At Long Last, when the Stenographers were Shewing Signs of Exhaustion, the Erudite Judge Reached the Conclusion that the Question was Admissible.

The Witness having Returned to the Box Counsel for the Plaintiff Once More Enquired: "What did the Charwoman Say when you Told her that the Plaintiff had Fallen Over the Pail on the Stairs?"

The Witness Replied that the Charwoman hadn't said Nothing. He Added that he wasn't Surprised, which the Charwoman was as Deaf as a Post.

Moral.—*Reserve Judgment*.

BOODLE, CASH & CO. AND THE BIG JOB

BOODLE, CASH & CO. AND THE
BIG JOB

∾

MR. BOODLE and Mr. Cash were the Senior Partners in the Firm of Boodle, Cash & Co. Various Sons and Nephews, who Showed Up at the Annual Share-Out, were the Co. If a Big Job came along it was Mr. Boodle and Mr. Cash who Tackled it. One Fine Day a Client of Immense Importance Blew In. He was in a State of Great Agitation. Millions were at Stake and he Insisted that the Best Brains at the Bar must be Secured for the Conduct of the Case.

Mr. Boodle and Mr. Cash Dined together the Same Evening to Decide which Eminent Counsel should be Retained. Mr. Boodle was all for Howler, K.C. Mr. Cash Thought Squeaker, K.C., was the Man for their Money. Mr. Boodle Pointed Out that Squeaker, K.C., was Inaudible, and that Howler, K.C., was a Magnificent Cross-Examiner. Mr. Cash Retorted that Howler, K.C., was Quarrelsome, while Squeaker, K.C., was a First-Class Lawyer. Finally Mr. Boodle and Mr. Cash Agreed that they had better Retain them Both.

Did Things go well? They did Not. When the Defendant had to be Cross-Examined, Howler, K.C., was Elsewhere, and when the Law had to be Expounded Squeaker, K.C., was Engaged in the Court of Appeal.

Moral.—*Don't Litigate.*

THE LEARNED YOUTH, UNCLE ROBERT
AND THE CONSULTATION

THE LEARNED YOUTH, UNCLE
ROBERT AND THE CONSULTATION

∽

ARE Virtue and Industry always Rewarded?
They are not. A Learned Youth was Once
Entrusted with a Difficult Matter. The Solici-
tor Instructing him was his Uncle Robert. The
Learned Youth Gave his Whole Mind to the Problems
Laid before him, and Advised, at length, as to (1) the
Cause of Action (if any); (2) the Party or Parties to be
Sued; (3) the Possibility of Enforcing a Judgment in
the Union of Socialist Soviet Republics; (4) whether
the Writ could be Served out of the Jurisdiction; and
(5) Generally. Later on the Learned Youth Pre-
pared a Statement of Claim of a very Imposing
Character. On the Eve of the Trial a Consultation
Took Place in the Chambers of the Great Man who
was to Lead the Learned Youth. The Lay Client,
Uncle Robert, and Everybody Else Attended.

When the Great Man Opened the Ball by An-
nouncing that in his Opinion the Action was Entirely
Misconceived, Uncle Robert Exhibited Symptoms of
Incipient Cerebral Hæmorrhage.

Was Uncle Robert Consoled when the Great Man,
after Listening Attentively to a Dissertation from the
Learned Youth, Humbly Admitted that the Learned
Youth had been Perfectly Right throughout? No.
Even after Judgment had been Recovered, with Costs,
Uncle Robert Continued to Think and Speak of the
Learned Youth as the Idiot who had Nearly Let him
Down.

Moral. *Relations are Readily Strained.*

MR. TOMPKYNS, CORINNE BOZIEU AND
THE CLOSE-UP

MR. TOMPKYNS, CORINNE BOZIEU
AND THE CLOSE-UP

～

MR. TOMPKYNS was all in a Twitter when he Heard that Corinne Bozieu, the Fascinating Vamp, Desired his Professional Assistance in the High Court of Justice. And when Mr. Tompkyns was Told that Corinne would herself Confer with him, his Excitement Knew no Bounds.

Corinne Duly Arrived at Sealing-Wax Buildings. Her Charming Appearance Filled Mr. Tompkyns with the Tenderest Emotion. Fixing her Lustrous Eyes upon Mr. Tompkyns, Corinne Told her Sad Story.

It seemed that she had Fallen Out with the Management and was Seeking Damages for Breach of Contract, Wrongful Dismissal, Slander, and Loss of Publicity. The Whole Trouble had Arisen over a Close-Up, and Corinne was Certain that if Anything had Gone Wrong it was All the Fault of that Silly Electrician.

Mr. Tompkyns Made Careful Notes as Corinne Proceeded with her Narrative, and (being a Prudent Person) Asked Corinne to Tell him what Exactly a Close-Up was.

Corinne Explained that the Gentleman Grasps the Lady's Left Arm with his Right Hand. Meanwhile he Spreads the Fingers of his Left Hand across her Shoulders. He then Draws the Lady in the Direction

349

of his Waistcoat and Embraces her Tenderly for Some Seconds.

Mr. Tompkyns, Greatly Interested, Said it would Assist him if he could have a Demonstration of a Close-Up, and Intimated that he was Quite Ready to Do the Gentleman's Part. With Becoming Modesty, he Added that he was Afraid Corinne would Find him Very Clumsy.

Corinne Agreed with Alacrity that this was an Excellent Idea, and Proposed, with a Delightful Little Laugh, that they should Ask her Chaperon (who was Waiting in the Clerk's Room) to Join them.

Mr. Tompkyns, though rather Disappointed to Find Corinne so Victorian in her Ideas, did not See his Way to Oppose this Proposition.

The Chaperon was Ushered in. She was Fat, Muscular, Elderly and Spectacled. To the Horror of Mr. Tompkyns, Corinne Ordered the Chaperon to Show Mr. Tompkyns how to Do a Close-Up.

Placing her Bag and Umbrella on the Table, the Chaperon Told Mr. Tompkyns to Come On. And as Mr. Tompkyns did not Do it Right the First Time, the Chaperon Made Mr. Tompkyns Repeat the Close-Up till he was Perfect.

Moral.—*Deal with the Principal.*

THE VOLUBLE PLAINTIFF AND THE
LACONIC INTERPRETER

THE VOLUBLE PLAINTIFF AND THE LACONIC INTERPRETER

~

ONCE Upon a Time there Appeared in the Royal Courts of Justice a Voluble Plaintiff of Foreign Extraction. His Country, which Owed its Origin to the Treaty of Versailles, was Situated in the Balkan Region. The Claim of the Voluble Plaintiff, which was both Large and Complicated, was Stoutly Resisted by the Defendant.

As the Voluble Plaintiff was Unacquainted with the English Language the Services of an Interpreter were Requisitioned. When The Time Came for his Cross-Examination, Counsel for the Defendant, by Way of Clearing the Decks, Asked the Voluble Plaintiff whether he had not some Three Years ago Made a Fraudulent Claim upon Underwriters. The Question having been Translated, the Voluble Plaintiff Gave a Shrill Scream Resembling that of a Locomotive Engine when Entering a Tunnel and Delivered an Eloquent Speech, in the Course of which he Threw his Arms about in a Terrifying Fashion. At the End of Five Minutes the Voluble Plaintiff Paused for Breath and the Judge Enquired of the Interpreter what the Voluble Plaintiff had said. The Interpreter Cleared his Throat and Replied: "'E Say 'No.'"

Moral.—*Keep it Short.*

THE KING OF THE UPPER AND LOWER
CANNIBAL ISLANDS AND THE REGIUS
PROFESSOR

THE KING OF THE UPPER AND
LOWER CANNIBAL ISLANDS AND
THE REGIUS PROFESSOR

∽

THE King of the Upper and Lower Cannibal Islands, being an Enlightened Monarch, Determined to Raise the Standard of his Local Legal Tribunals. To this End he Took the Opinions of the Jurists of Other Countries. Arriving in England he was Referred by the Colonial Office to a Regius Professor who had Made the Practice and Procedure of British Courts of Justice the Study of a Lifetime. The Regius Professor Explained to his Majesty that though the British System was an Expensive one it Happily Cost the Country Nothing. For Nobody could Assert or Defend a Claim without Paying through the Nose at Every Stage of the Proceedings. Thus the Litigants Unconsciously and Painlessly Provided the Cash for Heating and Lighting the Courts and Paying the Salaries of the Judges.

The British Courts, Proceeded the Regius Professor, were Famed for their Absolute Fairness. To Demonstrate their Impartiality they Extended Peculiar Indulgence to Blackmailers, Thieves and Lunatics, all of whom were Deemed to be Virtuous and Sane till the Contrary was Affirmatively Established. Further, it was well Understood that if a Defendant Failed to Appear when his Case was Called On, the

Plaintiff must Prove his Claim with the Utmost Strictness, the Presumption being that the Plaintiff was a Fraudulent Person.

Difficult Questions of Fact were Referred to a Jury of Twelve Reasonable Men and Women. If their Verdict Proved to be Entirely Unreasonable, a New Trial (with a Fresh Jury) was Ordered at the Expense of the Parties, in the Hope that a Different Result would be Secured.

When his Majesty Asked how Twelve Reasonable Persons could Arrive at an Unreasonable Verdict the Regius Professor said he would Deal with that Topic a little Later.

Questions of Law, the Regius Professor Mentioned, were Decided by a Judge from whom there was an Appeal to the Court of Appeal and to the House of Lords. An Appellant could not Succeed in the House of Lords unless he had a Majority in his Favour. Thus if their Lordships Chanced to be Equally divided the Appeal was Dismissed. His Majesty Enquired why the Appeal was not Heard Again, and the Regius Professor said he didn't Know. Divorce Cases, the Regius Professor Continued, were Usually Tried by Lawyers who had been Trained Exclusively in the Admiralty Court, for Reasons which he would Subsequently Explain; and Questions relating to the Cost and Quality of Female Garments were referred to Bachelor Judges. As at this Point the Regius Professor Seemed to be Running Down, his Majesty Thanked him Warmly and Observed that he Thought the System Obtaining in the Upper and Lower Cannibal Islands was, on the Whole, to be

Preferred. If, said His Majesty, a Plaintiff Succeeded in his Claim, the Defendant was at once Handed Over to him to be Eaten; and *Vice Versa*. If Claim and Counterclaim were both Dismissed, the Plaintiff and the Defendant were Reserved for Public Consumption on the Next National Holiday. His Majesty Thought, however, that the Plan of Making the Litigants Pay for the Courts and the Judges was a Good One.

Moral.—*Be Just.*

MR. PUMPKIN, K.C., M.P., THE PORTRAIT, AND
THE WEDDING BELLS

MR. PUMPKIN, K.C., M.P., THE PORTRAIT, AND THE WEDDING BELLS

～

TO Link Together Cause and Effect is not Always an Easy Matter. But there is no Doubt that the Brush of the Artist who Painted the Portrait of Mr. Pumpkin, K.C., M.P., Set the Wedding Bells Ringing.

Mr. Pumpkin, K.C., M.P., was an Elderly Gentleman whose Personal Appearance was on the Ordinary Side. His Features were Wanting in Regularity, and his Figure did not Recall that of the Eros now Happily Restored to Piccadilly Circus. He was accordingly Much Relieved when the Lady Artist (Cheap) who had been Commissioned by his Constituents to Paint his Portrait Produced a Very Pleasing Presentment of a Handsome Advocate in Wig and Gown. The Only Fear of Mr. Pumpkin, K.C., M.P., was that his Friends might Say that the Portrait was Unduly Flattering. Therefore, when his Friend Mrs. Plumply (Widow) Expressed the View that the Likeness was Excellent, but (if he would not Mind her Saying So) that the Artist had *Not* Done Justice to his Eyes, and that it was Positively *Wicked* to have Hidden his Beautifully shaped Head under a Wig, Mr. Pumpkin, K.C., M.P., Plucked Up Courage and Asked Mrs. Plumply to be his.

Moral.—*Lay It on Thick.*

359

MR. SPLASHER, K.C., AND THE BRIEF WHICH
WAS SUITABLY MARKED

MR. SPLASHER, K.C. AND THE BRIEF WHICH WAS SUITABLY MARKED

∽

DESIRING to Sue Various Officials of the Cats' Meat Distributors' Trade Union for Acts Done in Pursuance of an Alleged Illegal Conspiracy, an Aggrieved Person was Advised to Retain Mr. Splasher, K.C. He did so. Mr. Splasher, K.C., who was of the Conservative Faith, Held the View that Every Man has a Right to Work; but that he also has a Duty to Accept with Gratitude such Wages as his Employer Thinks he can Afford to Pay him. Mr. Splasher, K.C., also considered that Attempts by Workers to Raise the Rate of Wages by Artificial Means were Dishonest, and that the Modern Machinery of Trade Unionism was a Menace to the Social Structure. Accordingly Mr. Splasher, K.C., after Reading the Sad Story of the Aggrieved Person with a Sympathetic Eye, Composed some Telling Passages for his Opening Speech. When Leaving his Chambers Mr. Splasher, K.C., had a Few Words with his Clerk. He was Pleased to Learn from that Faithful Official that they had the Same Fee as the Other Side; that if the Other Side's Fee were Raised theirs was to be Pushed Up also; that the Special Fee (as Mr. Splasher, K.C., was not a Member of the Circuit) was Duly Marked; that a Refresher of a Hundred had been Agreed; and that their Junior had Got his Two-Thirds All Right.

Moral—*Down with the Reds.*

BEEFY AND BRAWN

BEEFY AND BRAWN

~

THAT Beefy of St. Polycarp's was the Best Six of his Time was Universally Admitted at Oxbridge; nor did Anybody at Camford Seriously Contend that a More Brilliant Stroke than Brawn of All Hallows' had Ever Shot Barnes Bridge. Small Wonder that Beefy and Brawn Represented their Respective Universities on Four Occasions, and that when they Retired from Aquatics there was General Lamentation in the World of Sport. Years Rolled by, and on a Chilly Morning in the Month of March Beefy of St. Polycarp's (now Mr. Justice Beefy) met Brawn of All Hallows' (now Chief Justice Brawn, K.C.I.E.) at Putney. They were about to Follow the Race on the Old Blues' Steamer. It was a Great Shock to Mr. Justice Beefy to Realise that while he himself had Retained All his Youthful Activity, Poor Old Brawn had Completely Gone to Seed. Chief Justice Brawn, K.C.I.E., Confessed the Same Evening to a Friend at the Club that Poor Old Beefy's Appearance had Greatly Distressed him. He had Never Seen such a Flat-Footed Old Elephant. Chief Justice Brawn, K.C.I.E., Added that he Failed to Understand why, if he himself could Remain Young and Active, Old Beefy Couldn't do so also.

Moral.—*Why Grow Old?*

363

THE TWO CLERKS WHO EXCHANGED
EXPERIENCES

THE TWO CLERKS WHO EXCHANGED
EXPERIENCES

∽

AN Aged and Retired Clerk, Revisiting the Glimpses of the Moon, Fell into Conversation with a Youthful Member of his Species. "Remember," said the Aged Clerk, "that you are a Person of no Little Importance to your Employer. I myself was Clerk to a Barrister who, but for my Exertions would never have been Heard of. He was, I Grieve to Say, Idle, Unbusinesslike and Ignorant, but by Dint of Unremitting Toil and Unfailing Tact I was Able to Seat him on the Woolsack." "Sir," Replied the Youthful Clerk, "What you tell me Matches my Relatively Short Experience. I am Junior Clerk to a City Solicitor of Considerable Eminence. His Success in the Profession is to me a Mystery, for he is Coarse in his Manners, and entirely Devoid of Intelligence. Indeed, Were it not for my Alertness and Devotion, the Whole Blinking Show would Bust Up." The Youthful Clerk then Hurried Away to Put Half a Crown on *Bumboat* for the Three-Thirty; and the Aged Clerk Looked at his Watch to See Whether the Houses of Entertainment were Still Closed.

Moral.—*Keep your Eye on Him.*

MR. JUSTICE SNAPPY AND JANE

MR. JUSTICE SNAPPY AND JANE

〜

MR. JUSTICE SNAPPY was the Terror of the Criminal Classes. When the News that he was Coming to the Old Bailey Reached the Cells of that Establishment the Lamentations of their Occupants were Loud and Long. For they were Confident that Protracted Periods of Penal Servitude, Accompanied (in Suitable Cases) by Heavy Doses of the Cat, were in Store for them. Nor did Mr. Justice Snappy Ever Disappoint their Expectations.

One Evening Mr. Justice Snappy, Whilst Awaiting the Sound of the Dinner-Gong, Reflected with Satisfaction that During the Working Day he had Handed Out to the Offenders who had Appeared before him One Hundred and Fifteen Years and Sixty-Four Lashes. His Meditations were Interrupted by Jane, his Younger Daughter, who Enquired in a Peremptory Manner whether he had Bought the Tickets for *"Hullo, Girls!"*

When Mr. Justice Snappy Replied in a Shaky Voice that he had Quite Forgotten to Do So, Jane Told him that his Conduct was Positively Putrid, that she was Absolutely Fed Up with him, and that he Ought to Have a Trained Nurse to Look After him.

Mr. Justice Snappy Trembled Violently and Said he was Very Sorry Indeed.

Moral.—*Warm Them Up.*

367

YOUNG MR. SIMPLE AND THE VENERABLE
SOLICITOR

YOUNG MR. SIMPLE AND THE VENERABLE SOLICITOR

∽

A VENERABLE Solicitor, Anxious to do Young Mr. Simple a Good Turn, Visited his Chambers for a Conference. Young Mr. Simple, Delighted to be Singled Out by so Eminent a Personage, Received the Venerable Solicitor with Respectful Cordiality and Begged to be Informed as to the Nature of the Problems by which he was Oppressed. With the Object of Telling a Clear and Vivid Story which would Readily be Followed by Young Mr. Simple, the Venerable Solicitor Assumed the Character of his Client. "I am," he said, "an Elderly Gentleman; I have a Large Town-House and a Handsome Place in The Country; my Income from Gilt-Edged Securities is a Comfortable One; but my Faculties are Waning." At this Point Young Mr. Simple Thought it well to Observe, in a Hearty and Reassuring Voice, that the Venerable Solicitor was Taking too Gloomy a View of his Mental Condition. And Young Mr. Simple to this Day does not Know why the Venerable Solicitor Leapt from his Chair, Uttered a Series of Horrid Maledictions, and Disappeared from his Chambers for Ever.

Moral.—*Don't Interrupt.*

MR. JUSTICE LIEN AND MR. JUSTICE DROP

MR. JUSTICE LIEN AND MR. JUSTICE DROP

～

M R. JUSTICE LIEN (Trained in the Commercial Court) and Mr. Justice Drop (Bred at the Old Bailey) Proceeded Hand-in-Hand to a Northern Assize Town. It was their First Circuit. Lien, J., who was in Charge of the Calendar, Found himself rather At Sea. Nor was Drop, J., at all Happy when he Got to Work on the Causes. Respectively Puzzled, Each Sought the Assistance of the Other.

Drop, J., was thus Enabled to Deliver a Masterly Judgment (Composed by his Brother Lien) on the York-Antwerp Rules and the Doctrine of Subrogation, while Lien, J., Read out to the Jury an Illuminating Dissertation (Drafted by his Brother Drop) on the Nature and Effect of Corroborative Evidence. Was the Result Satisfactory? Not Entirely. For the Court of Criminal Appeal Held without Hesitation that Lien, J., had Misdirected the Jury, and the Lords Justices were Unanimously Agreed that Drop, J., had Failed to Appreciate the Niceties of the Law of Marine Insurance. In the Judgments of both Tribunals it was Tactfully Suggested that Lien and Drop, JJ., had been Grappling Manfully with Unfamiliar Topics.

Moral.—*Cheats Never Prosper.*

THE OLD BUFFER WHO LIVED IN THE
TEMPLE

THE OLD BUFFER WHO LIVED IN
THE TEMPLE

&

THERE was once an Old Buffer who Occupied
a Fourth Floor in Plum-Tree Court. He
Always Wore a Top Hat. His Tenancy
Dated from 1871. In 1880 the Old Buffer, to his
Great Surprise, Received a Brief from a Solicitor (who
Thought he was Somebody Else); but, apart from
this Adventure, the Old Buffer's Professional Career
had been Inactive. The Old Buffer Dined Nightly
at the "Stilton Cheese," except during Term Time,
when he Fed in the Hall of the Outer Temple. Here
he would Tell his Next-Door Neighbour Stories of
the Tichborne Case. In 1890 the Old Buffer Began
to Write a Book about "The Six Clerks' Office," but
when the Great War Broke out he had not got beyond
Chapter III. Apart from his Laundress, of whom he
was Rather Afraid, the Old Buffer had no Friends.
During the Long Vacation he Found Things Rather
Dull.

In 1929 the Old Buffer Began to Exhibit Symptoms
of Senile Decay. When he Passed Away in 1930 the
Only Person who Regretted his Disappearance was a
Blind Beggar to whom he Gave Sixpence Every
Saturday Morning. The Undertaker's Men Found
the Stairs rather Troublesome. The Manuscript of
"The Six Clerks' Office" was Used by the Laundress
to Light the Fire for the Next Tenant.

The Old Buffer Left his Money to Trustees, Directing them to Establish a Home for Aged Cab-Horses. As these Animals were Found to be Extinct the Trustees Sought the Guidance of the Chancery Courts. The Society for the Befriending of Motherless Cats, the Association for the Housing of Homeless Mules, and the Society for the Promotion of Kindness to Pigs all Asked that the *Cy-Près* Doctrine should be Applied in their Favour, and the Proceedings were Protracted and Costly.

Ultimately it was held that Everything went to the Crown. When the Costs had been Paid Everything Amounted to 61*l*. 4*s*. 10*d*. (Sixty-one Pounds Four shillings and Tenpence).

Moral.—*Live in the Temple.*

APPENDIX

THE DISTINGUISHED BENCHER
AND THE LOST FABLE

With apologies to " O "

〰

THERE was Once a Distinguished Bencher of
Lincoln's Inn who Wrote and Illustrated
Forensic Fables.   In the Preface to the Third
Volume he Promised Not to Do it Again, a Promise
he Repeated (In Parentheses) in the Fourth Volume in
1932.   Shortly Afterwards he Took Dinner in Hall.
His Menu, after Unknown Adventures, was Discovered in 1961 Tucked into a Second-hand Volume,
and is Here Reproduced.   If the Text is Obscure
the Illustrations are Graphic and Characteristic.

Moral.—*Don't Draw on the Menu.*

LINCOLN'S INN HALL.

The Rt. Hon. Lord BLANESBURGH, G.B.E., Treasurer.

MENU.

BENCH TABLE.

Clear Soup.

Fillet Sole, Meunière

...

Mutton Cutlet. Reform.

Persillée Potato, French Beans.

...

Cold Chicken, Ham, or Tongue.

Green Salad.

Fruit Savarin.

Cheese.

Coffee.

...

377

INDEX

A

379

387

BUFFER,

C
CAB,

389

393

394

397

E

EMERITUS PROFESSOR (*continued*)
 published works of, 147
 spectacles of, 147
 weak voice of, 147

EMPHYTEUTIC LEASE,
 case concerning, 31

EMOTION,
 of Tearful Performer, 116

ENGAGEMENT,
 long, insisted upon, 238
 short, insisted upon, 238

ENGINE,
 locomotive, 353

ENGLISH LAKES,
 visited by Enthusiastic Tourists, 181

ENQUIRIES,
 made by Industrious Youth, 84

ENTERTAINMENT,
 houses of, closed, 365

ENTHUSIASTIC,
 Beginner, briefed in Privy Council, 31
   contempt of, for Leader, 31
   determination of, to follow Leader, 31
   second thoughts of, 32
 Tourists, address of Capable Guide to, 181
   crowded fortnight of, 181
   largesse heaped upon Capable Guide by, 181
   visit of, to Temple, 181

EPILEPTIC FIT. *See* FIT

EQUITY,
 Draftsmen, luncheon of, 19
   noisy behaviour of, 19
   old brandy consumed by, 19
   stories told by, 19
   And see AGED CONVEYANCERS
 Leader. *See* LEADER

403

405

409

JOKE,
   ancient, alluded to by Elderly Conveyancers, 19
   enthusiastic reception of, 35
   made by Counsel, 35
   prepared by Witty Judge, 35
JONES, MISS,
   attraction of Elderly Junior towards, 27
   eyes of, 27
   figure of, 27
   reference of, to Aunt Jane, 28
   tripping off of, 28
   visit of, to Elderly Junior, 27
   well-shaped hand of, 28
JUDÆA,
   Caledonian from, 70
JUDGE,
   aged. *See* JUDGE, AGED
   boredom of, 23
   Chancery. *See* JUDGE, CHANCERY
   congratulations to, by Lord Chancellor, 24
   doze of, 23
   Erudite. *See* JUDGE, ERUDITE
   kindly. *See* JUDGE, KINDLY
   of Assize. *See* JUDGE OF ASSIZE
      Caledonian extraction, 69
   old-fashioned. *See* JUDGE, OLD-FASHIONED
   presence of mind, 24
   profound sleep of, 23
   prudent. *See* JUDGE, PRUDENT
   questions of, to Holder in Due Course, 4
   relations of, with Marshal, 51
   stay of execution granted by, 24
                     refused by, 70
JUDGE, AGED,
   fruitful kindness of, 202
   hints of, disregarded, 201
   irritation of, 201
   past remembered by, 201
   tears of, 202
   untruthful compliment paid by, 201

413

414

JURY (*continued*)
    unable to agree, 232
    withdrawal of, ordered, 341

JUSTICE,
    emblematical figure of, 310
    Palace of, burning of, 217
                defects of, 217
                rebuilding of, 218
    spirit of, invoked, 306

JUSTINIAN,
    Pandects of, 341

K

K.C. M.P.,
    bill for suppression of night clubs of, 91
        paid by, 91
    dancing lessons given to, by Madame Frou-Frou, 91
    explanation to police by, 92
    mingling with orchestra of, 92
    scrapping of bill by, 92
    successful ballot of, 91
    supper taken by, with lady member, 91
    visit of, to "Bubble and Squeak," 91
                "Giddy Goat," 91
                "Pongo's," 91
                "Tiddlywinks," 91
    wig and moustache hired by, 91

KASHMIRI,
    tongue, 193

KENSINGTON GARDENS,
    perambulator upset in, 49

KHOJAS,
    laws and customs of, 193

KING OF UPPER AND LOWER CANNIBAL ISLANDS,
    enlightenment of, 355
    explanation of local legal procedure by, 356, 357
    preference expressed by, 356, 357
    referred to Regius Professor, 355
    Regius Professor's lecture to, 355, 356

418

419

M

423

429

430

436

SHOCK,
> to Traveller, 49

SHRIMPTON-ON-SEA,
> visited, 337

SHROPSHIRE,
> clergyman in, 242
>> marriage of, 242

SILK, *and see* LEADER
> absence of, in other Court, 1
> application for, by Utter Barrister, 62
> brief lost by, 21
> cheered by arrival of client, 21
> confidential communication of, to Zealous Clerk, 21
> consultation with, 222, 279
> masterly performance of, 222
> various appointments of, 21
> wink of, 21
> world-wide fame of, 279

SIMPLE, YOUNG MR.,
> conference between, and Venerable Solicitor, 369
> hearty voice of, 369

SIMPLICITY,
> of Sagacious Cook, 331

SIR JOHN, 21

SIR NATHANIEL, 45

SIR PEREGRINE, 45

SIX,
> Beefy best, of his time, 363

SIX CLERKS' OFFICE,
> history of, 373

SIXPENCE,
> tendered by Real Property Lawyer, 80

SLANDER,
> claim and counterclaim for, 45

SLASHER, MR.,
> beautiful iron shot of, 119
> down in nine at eighteenth, 120

444

446

447

448

454